THE GOLD GUIDES

VIENNA

A VISITOR'S GUIDE TO THE CITY

DISCOVER THE CITY'S HISTORICAL
MONUMENTS AND ART

NEW ED

Distributor
for Austria:
VERLAG C.BAUER GmbH
Beatrixgasse 3
1030 WIEN

Publication created and designed by: Casa Editrice Bonechi;
Editorial management: Alberto Andreini; Graphic design, layout and cover: Elena Nannucci;
Editing: Elena Rossi; Texts: new edition revised in 2006 by the Casa Editrice Bonechi editorial staff;
Translation: Paula Elise Boomsliter; Maps and drawings: Stefano Benini (p.78-79, 88-89),
Sauro Giampaia (p. 12-13, 18 bottom).

© Copyright by Casa Editrice Bonechi - Florence - Italy
E-mail: bonechi@bonechi.it

The photographs are property of the Casa Editrice Bonechi Archives, with the exception of:
The photographs on pages 7, excepting the timeline photos, 20, 21, 27 top left, 27 bottom, 28, 29, 31 top,
37 top, 40, 41 bottom, 46 top, 47 top right, 47 center, 47 bottom left, 53 top, 53 center, 56 top, 58 top, 59
bottom, 62, 64 top, 64 center, 69 (photo by H. Popelka), 76 bottom, 77 bottom left, 83 top, 85 top, 85 bottom
(photo by B. Koch), 88 (photo of the Riesenrad), 90/91, 98 center, 98 bottom right, 99 top right, 99 center
left, 102 center, 106 top, 108 bottom, 113 first photograph top right, 117 bottom right, 120 bottom, 120/121
and 121 top (photo by H. Popelka), 123 bottom, 124 top, 124 bottom right, and 128 top are used by the kind
permission of Verlag Bauer GmbH, Wien. Bundesministerium für Land- und Forstwirtschaft: p. 50 bottom;
Historisches Museum der Stadt Wien: p. 5 top, 8 bottom right, 27 top right, 56 center right, 104 top, 105 top
left; Kunsthandlung Entzmann Wien: p. 33 bottom; Kunsthistorisches Museum Wien: p. 4 bottom right, 7 two
timeline photos on the right, 71, 80 bottom, 86 center; Museum für Angewandte Kunst (Photo Gerald Zugmann):
p. 98 top; Naturhistorisches Museum Wien: p. 72, 73; Private Archives: p. 5 center, 38; Private Collection: p.
56 center left, 105 top right; Sammlungen der Gesellschaft der Musikfreunde in Wien: p. 60 top; Spanische
Hofreitschule: p. 51; Universitätsbibliothek, Heidelberg: p. 5 bottom; Vienna Boys Choir: p. 43 bottom; Wiener
Tourismusverband: p. 107. The photograph on page 9 bottom right is kindly provided by Leopold Museum, Wien.
The photographs on pages 111-112 are kindly provided by Liechtenstein Museum, Wien.

We apologize in advance for any unintentional errors or omissions. We would be pleased to include appropriate
acknowledgements in any subsequent edition of this publication and to pay any royalties due to legitimate
copyright holders.

ISBN 978-88-476-1965-4

www.bonechi.com

INTRODUCTION

VIENNA TODAY

*V*ienna is one of central Europe's most beautiful capital cities.
The visitor is invariably enchanted by the great artistic heritage
of the city, where a wealth of monuments testifying to Viennese
history and culture are concentrated in a relatively small area.
The visitor to the city will discover Imperial Vienna, with palaces
and parks that recall the splendor of the
Hapsburg dynasty, the spectacular Ring
with its shops, magnificent churches, beginning with the Stephansdom cathedral, and
numerous museums preserving artworks
and treasures of immeasurable value—like
the Kunsthistorisches Museum. Vienna was
one of the capitals of European Jugendstil,
and examples this style are to be found all
over the city: outstanding are the Secession
Building and the Linke Wienzeile, with several buildings by Otto Wagner, one of the
maximum exponents of this artistic current.
But Vienna is also a future-looking city, as
we see in the many innovative urban planning and architectural
solutions and in the dynamism of the culture and lifestyle of its
young people. The outskirts of the city offer a multitude of opportunities for pleasurable excursions; for example, a romantic stroll
through the Vienna Woods or an outing to a Heurige for a taste of
the young local wines.

The best way to see Vienna is on foot, but a bike tour is an excellent alternative: the city boasts a first-rate network of cycle paths and routes especially designed to help you discover the city with this means of transport. Another enjoyable and very relaxing way of discovering Vienna is to ride in one of the typical Fiaker, the traditional horse-drawn open carriages.

A stop at one of the many coffeehouses is *de rigueur* on any trip to Vienna. These establishments are conventional meeting places where you can spend a pleasant hour enjoying a snack or a slice of the characteristic Sachertorte accompanied by one of the many different types of coffee for which the cafés are famous.

TIMELINE – HIS

First permanent settlements in the Vienna area

The town is rebuilt and Marcus Aurelius makes it his headquarters; the emperor dies in Vindobona in 180

| 3500-1800 BC. | 400 BC ca | 15 BC | 166 AD | 167-180 |

Neolithic Age — **Roman Period**

Celtic settlement of **Vindobona** on the site of today's Leopoldsberg

Under Emperor Augustus, the Romans establish a garrison of the same name on the south bank of the Danube

Vindobona destroyed by the Marcomanni

ENTERTAINMENT

Vienna offers the visitor a vast range of entertainment, above all musical. The city where the greatest Austrian musicians performed

(Haydn, Mozart, the Strauss' father and son, Berg, and many others) is renowned for its concerts and marvelous opera productions at the Staatsoper and at the Theater an der Wien. Important musical and theatrical events, like the Wiener Festwochen, from mid-May to mid-June, or the famous Viennese Carnival, featuring orchestra concerts and waltz music, are held with an annual cadence. Dance and waltz enthusiasts will not want to miss the legendary Viennese balls and in particular the Opera Ball for debutantes held during Carnival and the Kaiserball (Imperial Ball) on New Year's Eve.

Above, a public ball in Vienna in a painting by Wilhelm Gause, 1906. Two cover pages of piano adaptations of well-known operettas.

T O R Y   O F   V I E N N A

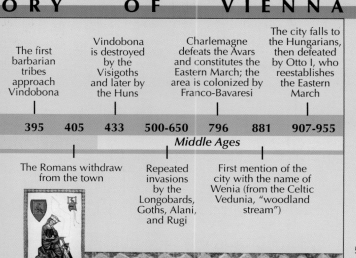

The first barbarian tribes approach Vindobona		Vindobona is destroyed by the Visigoths and later by the Huns		Charlemagne defeats the Avars and constitutes the Eastern March; the area is colonized by Franco-Bavaresi		The city falls to the Hungarians, then defeated by Otto I, who reestablishes the Eastern March
395	405	433	500-650	796	881	907-955
			Middle Ages			
The Romans withdraw from the town		Repeated invasions by the Longobards, Goths, Alani, and Rugi		First mention of the city with the name of Wenia (from the Celtic Vedunia, "woodland stream")		

VIENNA FOR THE YOUNGER SET

Vienna is one of the top-ranking European cities with young people. The Ring and the city center host unnumbered nightspots in which to spend many an entertaining evening, and bars, jazz clubs, discos, and casinos with live music. Particularly populated is the MuseumsQuartier area, where entertainment meets art and culture; Spittelberg is another district abounding in night spots, restaurants, and coffeehouses. Yet another area where the night life buzzes is the Bermudadreieck, the "Bermuda Triangle" where in a radius of just a few meters you'll find myriad cultural clubs and music bars.

The Gürtel area, the peripheral band uniting the north and south of the city, also hosts many popular venues.

In the U-Bahn arcades, designed by Otto Wagner, many spaces are occupied by trendy night spots, where the rhythms of rock, pop, and techno music mix for intellectuals, artists, and avant-garde musicians.

TIMELINE – HIS

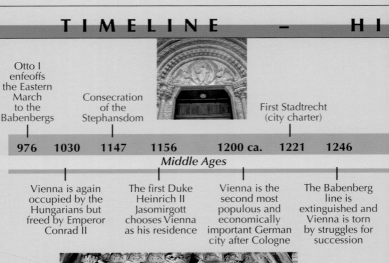

Otto I enfeoffs the Eastern March to the Babenbergs		Consecration of the Stephansdom			First Stadtrecht (city charter)	
976	1030	1147	1156	1200 ca.	1221	1246

Middle Ages

Vienna is again occupied by the Hungarians but freed by Emperor Conrad II	The first Duke Heinrich II Jasomirgott chooses Vienna as his residence	Vienna is the second most populous and economically important German city after Cologne	The Babenberg line is extinguished and Vienna is torn by struggles for succession

VIENNA FOR CHILDREN

Austria's capital also offers many attractions for the youngest set. A large number of city parks have play areas, and a visit to the funfair on the Prater, Vienna's most famous park, is a must.

And if your children think that trips to museums are boring, they'll change their minds in Vienna.

First of all, there's the Zoom Museum in the MuseumsQuartier, which features various sections where children from zero to fourteen will enjoy interactive experiences on themes from art, science, and daily culture.

Children will also certainly enjoy a visit to the Doll and Toy Museum and to the Teddybären Museum, where, as the name implies, they'll see antique toy bears of all conceivable types.

The show put on by the Lipizzan horses of the Spanish Riding School is especially fascinating, as is the interesting Lipizzaner Museum. Another not-to-be-missed attraction is a visit to one of the world's oldest zoos, in the Schönbrunn Palace gardens, to see both wild beasts and the domestic animals of the Tyrolese farms.

TORY   OF   VIENNA

Rudolf I Hapsburg becomes ruler of Austria; Hapsburg rule begins and the Gothic style flourishes in Vienna

Vienna is occupied by King Matthias Corvinus of Hungary; the city is retaken by Maximilian I in 1490

Empress Maria Teresa comes to the throne; under her and her son Joseph II's rules Vienna enjoys a long period of economic and cultural prosperity

1282	1365	1485-1490	1529	1683	1740-1780
		Renaissance		*17th c.*	*18th c.*

Founding of Vienna's University

First siege of Vienna by Suleiman II's Turks

Second Turkish siege

7

SHOPPING IN VIENNA

Vienna's main shopping district is the historical center, and in particular the pedestrian island bounded by Kärntner Strasse, the Graben, and the Kohlmarkt. Less elegant is Mariahilfer Strasse, the city's longest street dedicated to commerce, where the large department stores are concentrated. Among the most sought-after articles are the hand-painted porcelains manufactured at the Augarten castle since 1718, jewelry, crystal-ware (and in particular, Swarovski crystal), artistic ceramics, and handmade dolls; in clothing, the typical jackets, overcoats, and capes in Loden, a very warm fabric similar to felt, in dark green or grey.

The Austrian capital is also renowned for its many antique shops. located mainly near the Dorotheum, the city's most important auction house. In these shops you'll find, above all, furniture and other objects in Biedermeier style, in great demand by aficionados of central European culture.

TIMELINE – HIS

Congress of Vienna: a new European order is defined following the Napoleonic Wars		End of the Austro-Hungarian Empire; declaration of the Austrian Republic with Vienna as capital	Vienna suffers grave damage during Allied bombings: the Stefansdom, the Staatsoper, and the Ferris wheel on the Prater are destroyed; the city is divided into four zones

1814-1815   **1848**   **1918**   **1938**   **1945**
19th c.

In March, revolution of Vienna's populace; Franz Joseph, destined to give a new face to Vienna, comes to the throne

Vienna loses its role as capital and Austria becomes a province of the German Reich

Vienna's largest marketplace is the Naschmarkt. Here you'll find exotic fruit, vegetables, spices, tea, and Greek, Turkish, and Asian specialties. This market is a meeting-place for people of different nationalities; strolling among the stalls and absorbing its multi-ethnic atmosphere is a fascinating experience. But don't miss the Flohmarkt (flea market) either. It is one of the continent's largest, where you'll find everything imaginable: silverware, prints, porcelain, curios of all kinds, medals, and thousands of other objects. In the winter holiday period Vienna is dotted with Christmas markets whose vendors sell local crafts products and gift items.

Signing of the Austrian State Treaty: Vienna is capital of the new Austrian Federal Republic

Death of Empress Zita, the last Hapsburg ruler

Opening of the MuseumsQuartier

| 1955 | 1979 | 1989 | 1992 | 2001 |

20th c.   *21st c.*

Vienna is the third UNO city after New York and Geneva

Fire in the Hofburg; the Redoutensäle are destroyed

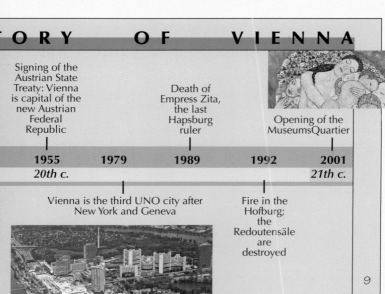

9

8ITINERARIES through VIENNA

We have divided the panorama of artistic, cultural and historical attractions offered by the City of Vienna into 8 different itineraries, each of which may be completed in a morning's or an afternoon's time.

Each walk will take the tourist through the one of most interesting areas of the city; the guide points out the most famous monuments, churches, museums, and patrician homes as well as little-known facts and the typical and singular aspects of each. The sights that must absolutely not be missed are printed in boldface for easy reference by the especially harried tourist.

I - p. 14
Stephansdom (Saint Stephan's Cathedral) - Stephansplatz (Saint Stephan's Square) - **Graben** - **Am Hof** - Uhrenmuseum (Clock Museum) - **Freyung** - Schottenkirche (Scottish Church) - Freyung-Passage.

II - p. 34
Michaelerplatz - **Hofburg** - Michaelertrakt - **Kaiserappartements** (State Apartments) - **"In der Burg"** - Amalienburg - Leopoldinischer Trakt - Reichskanzleitrakt - Alte Burg - Burgkapelle (Imperial Chapel) - **Weltliche und Geistliche Schatzkammer** (Sacred and Secular Treasuries) - Heldenplatz - Neue Burg - Neue Hofburg Museums - Hofburg Gardens - Schmetterlinghaus (Butterfly House) - Stallburg - Josefsplatz - Nationalbibliothek (National Library) - **Spanische Hofreitschule** (Spanish Riding School) - Augustinerkirche (Augustinian Church) - Albertina.

III - p. 54
Staatsoper - Hotel Sacher - **Kärntner Strasse** - **Kaisergruft** (Imperial Crypt) - Stadtpalais des Prinzen Eugen (Winter Palace of Prince Eugene) - Franziskanerkirche (Franciscan Church) - Mozarthaus (House of Mozart) - Dominikanerkirche (Dominican Church) - Schönlaterngasse - Heiligenkreuzerhof - Bernhardskapelle (Chapel of Saint Bernard) - Jesuitenkirche (Jesuit Church) - Akademie der Wissenschaften (Academy of Sciences) - Alte Universität - **Hoher Markt** - **Altes Rathaus** - Böhmische Hofkanzlei - Judenplatz - **Maria am Gestade** (Church of Saint Mary on the Bank) - Fleischmarkt - **Ruprechtskirche** (Church of Saint Ruprecht).

IV - p. 66
Ringstrasse - Äusseres Burgtor - Maria-Theresien-Platz - **Muse-umsQuartier** (Museum Quarter) - **Kunsthistorisches Museum** (Museum of the History of Art) - Naturhistorisches Museum (Museum of Natural History) - Parliament - Pallas-Athene-Brunnen (Fountain of Athena Pallas) - **Burgtheater** - **Rathaus** (City Hall) - Rathauspark - Universität - Votivkirche - Minoritenplatz - Minoritenkirche (Church of the Friars Minor).

V - p. 78
Schloss Schönbrunn (Schönbrunn Castle) - **Kaiserliche Appartements** (Imperial Apartments) - **Park** - Tiergarten (Zoological Garden) - Botanischer Garten (Botanical Garden) - Palmenhaus (Palm House) - **Wagenburg** (Imperial Coach Museum) - Technisches Museum (Technical Museum).

VI - p. 88
Unteres Belvedere (Lower Belvedere) - Österreichisches Barockmuseum (Museum of Austrian Baroque Art) - **Belvedere Park** - **Oberes Belvedere** (Upper Belvedere) - Österreichische Galerie des 19. und 20. Jahrhunderts (Museum of 19th- and 20th-Century Art) - Stadtpark - Kursalon - Wienflussportal (Portal of the River Wien) - **Museum für Angewandte Kunst** (Austrian Museum of Applied Arts) - Postsparkasse (Austrian Post Office Savings Bank) - Urania - **Prater.**

VII - p. 100
Karlskirche (Church of Saint Charles Borromeo) - Karlsplatz - **Wien Museum Karlsplatz** - Musikvereinsgebäude (Society of the Friends of Music Building) - Künstlerhaus (Artists' House) - Historische Stadtbahnstationen (Historical Underground Pavilions) - **Secession** (Sezession Building) - Akademie der Bildenden Künst (Academy of Fine Arts) - **Linke Wienzeile** - Theater an der Wien - Naschmarkt - Flohmarkt (Flea Market) - Majolikahaus - Spittelberg - Barockhaus am Ulrichsplatz - Bäckereimuseum (Bakery Museum) - Piaristenkirche Maria Treu (Piarist Church) - Palais Liechtenstein - **Liechtenstein Museum** - Josephinum - Sigmund Freud-Haus.

VIII - p. 113
Heeresgeschichtliches Museum (Museum of Army History) - Hundertwasserhaus - **St. Marxer Friedhof** (Saint Marx Monumental Cemetery) - **Zentralfriedhof** (Central Cemetery) - Kirche am Steinhof - Karl Marx-Hof - UNO-City (United Nations City) - Donau City - Donaupark - Donauturm (Danube Tower) - Heurigen.

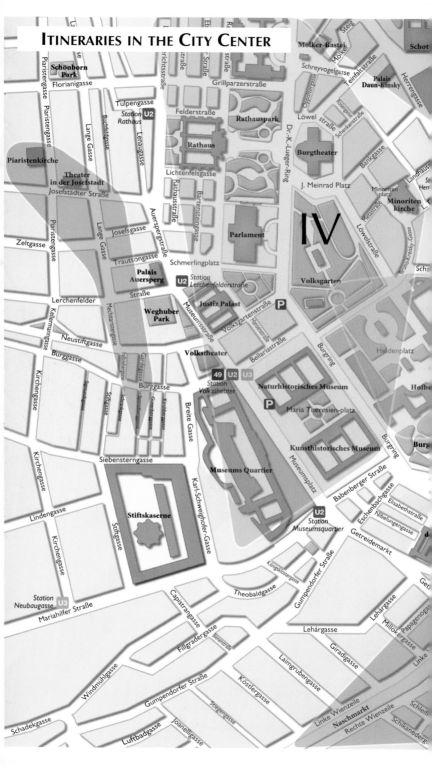

ITINERARIES IN THE CITY CENTER

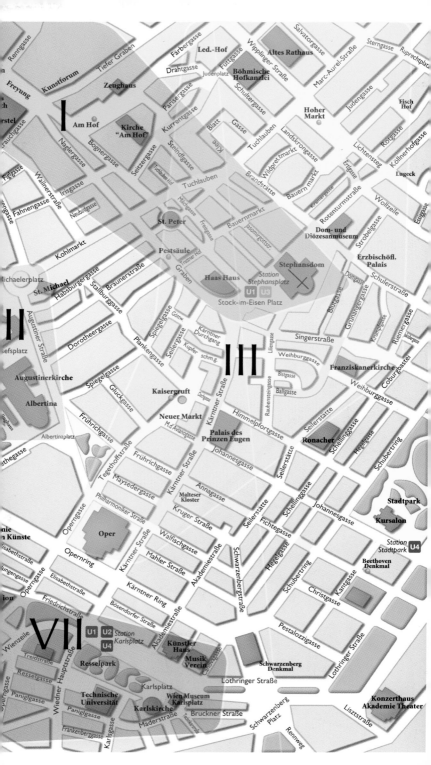

Palais Daun–Kinsky
• p. 30

Schottenkirche
• p. 31

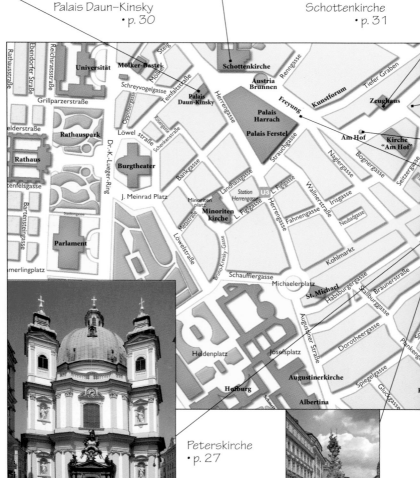

Peterskirche
• p. 27

Graben
• p. 26

Zeughaus • p. 29

ITINERARY I

Stephansdom
(Saint Stephan's Cathedral) –
Stephansplatz (Saint Stephan's
Cathedral) –
Graben – Am Hof –
Uhrenmuseum (Clock Museum) –
Freyung –
Schottenkirche (Scottish Church) –
Freyung-Passage

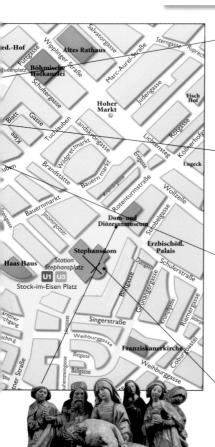

Clock Museum • p. 29

Am Hof • p. 28

Freyung
and the Freyung-Passage
• p. 30/32

Stephansdom • p. 16

Stephansplatz, Diocesan Museum
• p. 25

STEPHANSDOM

In the third decade of the 12th century, the Bishop of Passau ordered construction of the first Romanesque parish church on the site. Consecrated by him in 1147, it was a little smaller than the nave of today's Saint Stephan's Cathedral. Rebuilding was delayed on account of the fire that devastated the city in 1258 and was completed only in 1263, during the Interregnum.
Duke Albrecht I began construction of the Gothic choir (1304-1340) as it appears today.

The Stephansdom.

The first stone of the Gothic nave was laid in 1359 by Rudolf IV the Founder, while the South Tower, completed in 1433, was being built. Work on the North Tower, which was never completed, continued from 1450 through 1511.

In 1469, under Emperor Friedrich III, Vienna became a bishopric and the Stephansdom the diocesan church.

The various 17th-century reconstructions in Baroque style did not succeed in radically altering the original Gothic aspect of the Cathedral.

In April 1945, in the last days of World War II, the Stephansdom caught fire during bombing. Long and painstaking restoration work, carried out thanks to funding provided by all the Austrian regions and terminated only in 1956, returned the Cathedral all its ancient splendor.

The massive, compact form of the Cathedral, with an external length of 107 meters and a height at the roof ridge of 60 meters, is softened by the two Heidentürme.

The splendid colored tile roof, which was originally supported by larch wood beams and was completely destroyed in 1945, has been rebuilt in steel.

Detail of the roof of the Stephansdom.

The Stephansdom with the two Heidentürme (Heathen Towers).

West Façade - The **Riesentor** (Giants' Doorway) and the two compact side towers, called the **Heidentürme** (Heathen Towers) are all that remain of the original Romanesque church. The Riesentor is decorated with geometrical figures, animal motifs and the images of saints. Special mention must be made of the small figures in the left-hand corner: the *Steinmetz* (stonecutter) and *Saint Peter* bearing a large key. In the tympanum is a *Seated Christ* with His left knee uncovered, the Book of Life in His hand and two angels at the sides. This sculpted relief has been the subject of much discussion among art historians, some of whom argue that the uncovered knee alludes to the Masonic rite by which new initiates participated in the ceremony with their knee bared. On the façade are also found Romanesque sculptures, including, to the right of the doorway, a griffin and *Samson and the Lion*. To the right of the Riesentor we note the number "05" carved in 1945 to symbolize the Austrian Resistance Movement against National Socialism and annexation of Austria to Hitler's Germany. The number 5 signifies the fifth letter of the alphabet, and therefore 05 = OE = Oesterreich.

Christ Imparting the Blessing. *Detail of the Reisentor (Giants' Doorway).*

Exterior - On the right of the Cathedral (south side) is the **Singertor** (Singers' Gate), by Hans Puchsbaum, with a Gothic portal dating to 1440-1445. This door, decorated with many statues and sculpted reliefs, is comparable to the Riesentor for beauty. To the right, a niche contains the *statue of Rudolf IV the Founder* holding in his hand a model of the choir (built between 1304 and 1340) with the two planned towers.

Further ahead, we come to the Baroque Untere Sakristei (Lower Sacristy) over which there rises the slender, beautiful **South Tower** ("**Steffl**," as it is affectionately called by the Viennese). The many-spired

The relief sculptures on the Reisentor. The statue of Rudolf IV the Founder.

tower, 136.7 meters in height, is a valuable masterpiece of Gothic architecture that owes its elegant form to its peculiar structure: the tower, as it rises from the square base, becomes octagonal. Inside, a spiral staircase of 343 steps leads to the so-called Türmerstube (Bell-Ringer's Room) offering a splendid view of the city.

All around the apse of the church are 15th- and 16th-century reliefs as well as a numerous statues and the 15th-century **Capistrankanzel** (Capistrano

The tympanum of the Singertor (Singers' Gate).

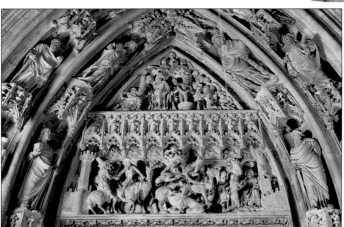

View of the interior of the Stephansdom.

Pulpit) from which Saint Johannes Capistrano preached in favor of a crusade against the Turks in 1451. The 15th-century statue of the *Schmerzensmann* (*Ecce Homo*) is striking. According to popular tradition, the statue (the original of which is in the left transept at the entrance to the crypt, while that in the church proper is only a copy), irreverently called "Christ with a Toothache," was donated to the Cathedral by a sinner cured of a toothache and later converted.

On the north side of the Cathedral is the unfinished tower called the **Nordturm** (North Tower). It terminates at 60.6 meters above street level with a Renaissance roof by the ar-

The exterior of the Stephansdom: the Capistrankanzel (Capistrano Pulpit).

chitect Hans Saphoy (1556-1578). The *Pummerin*, one of the world's largest bells, hangs in this tower: formed of 21,000 kg of bronze from Turkish cannons, the bell was recast after it was destroyed in 1945. An elevator takes us comfortably to the terrace of the tower to admire both the bell and the city panorama.

Interior - In the interior of the church, with its richly-decorated nave and two aisles, all of equal size, elements in Gothic style unite with the Baroque to create a harmonious and utterly fascinating composition. The magnificent vault and the imposing columns are illuminated by the large windows, the original colored glass panes of which were destroyed in 1945. We will begin our tour of the Cathedral from the right aisle: in the **Herzogs-kapelle** (Ducal Chapel) or Chapel of Saint Elijah, a *statue of the Virgin Mary* dating to the 14th century merits attention. Under a canopy built between 1510 and 1515, illuminated by some hundred votive candles, is the miraculous image of the *Pócs Madonna*, a painted icon from the Hungarian village of Pócs placed in the chapel in 1697.

On a level with the transept is the entrance to the **Untere Sakristei**, an 18th-century Baroque addition with ceiling paintings by Altomonte.

The most valuable works in the Cathedral are found in the nave. The **Kanzel** (pulpit) by an anonymous sculptor, against the third column on the right, is an incomparable masterpiece of Gothic art.

The figures of the *Four Fathers of the Church* (Augustine, Gregory, Jerome, Ambrose) representing the temperaments, and the richness of the detail on the pulpit as a whole make this work a

The cathedral pulpit.
Facing page: the Four Fathers of the Church *on the parapet of the pulpit; bottom left, the* Fensterguncker, *a self-portrait of the pulpit's anonymous sculptor; bottom right, Pilgram's self-portrait sculpted on the corbel of the organ.*

harmonious jewel unique in its genre. The so-called *Fenstergucker* (Window-Gazer), is the self-portrait of its anonymous creator with which he "signed" his work: a masterpiece within a masterpiece.

Further along, together with a number of Baroque works, is the *Dienstbotenmadonna* (Madonna of the Servants) from the early 14th century. Legend has it that the work was donated by a noblewoman who had unjustly accused her chambermaid of theft.

At the beginning of the left aisle, closed off by a beautiful Baroque gate adorned with the coats-of-arms of the Savoias and the Liechtensteins, is the **Tirnakapelle** or **Kreuzkapelle** (Tirna Chapel or Chapel of the Cross) with the *tomb of Prince Eugene of Savoia*, the hero who repulsed the Turks from central Europe. Alongside is the beautiful *15th-century Gothic canopy* by Hans Prachatitz. Almost at the end of the aisle is a work by Pilgram: the 1513 organ base is a statue of the master craftsman himself (a "self-portrait") holding a square and compass. The organ has long since been moved.

In the left transept is the **Crypt**, a simple room dating to 1752 and leading to the Catacombs, where since 1951 the mortal remains of the Archbishops of Vienna are entombed. In 1363, Rudolf IV ordered construction, in these subterranean vaults, of a crypt for the Dukes of Hapsburg. This was enlarged in 1754, during the reign of Maria Theresa, to house the copper urns containing the entrails of the members of the Hapsburg family; the embalmed corpses instead rest in the Kapuzinergruft (Capuchin Crypt) and the hearts in the Augustinerkirche (Augustinian Church).

The nave-and-two-aisle layout is repeated in the apsed choir. To the right, the **Apostelchor** (Apostles' Choir), with the *red marble tomb of Emperor Friedrich III,* is a fundamental work of the late Gothic funerary art of Niklas Gerhaert van Leyden, the most important Dutch sculptor of the time. Begun in 1469, it was unfinished at the time of both the artist's and the Emperor's deaths. Over the high altar at the end of the center choir, Tobias Pock's Baroque altarpiece (1667) depicts the *Lapidation of Saint Stephan.*

R·D·I·C·R

23

The **Frauenchor** (Women's Gallery) closes off the left transept with the Gothic *Wiener Neustädter Altarpiece* (1447) sculpted with scenes from the life of the Virgin Mary. It was brought here from Wiener Neustadt in 1883 and installed in its present location in 1952. To the left is the *funeral monument to Rudolf IV and his wife Catherine of Bohemia* (ca. 1360/65).

Above, the Wiener Neustädter Altarpiece *and the* Madonna of the Servants. *The High Altar by Johann Jakob Pock and Tobias Pock (1667).*

STEPHANSPLATZ

Stephansplatz (Saint Stephan's Square) encircles the Cathedral; its present-day aspect dates to the 18th century and the square has gained in beauty since being included in the pedestrian zone.

Before leaving the square, we suggest entering the U-bahn station to visit the remains of the **Virgil-Kapelle** (Chapel of Saint Virgil). This is an authentic 13th-century crypt in the cemetery that until 1783 surrounded the cathedral; it was "discovered" during the excavation work for building the underground. At the chapel is also a collection of vases and other archaeological finds brought to light during the excavations.

Facing the cathedral, to the left, a *Fiaker* stand awaits those whose program includes a romantic carriage-ride. The most noteworthy buildings on the square are the **Churhaus** (Curia) at No. 3, built between 1738 and 1740, the **Domher-ren-Hof** (Priest's Lodge) at No. 5, and the **Dom- und Diözesan-museum** (Cathedral and Diocesan Museum) at No. 6. In the Treasury and in five other rooms, this museum displays precious paintings, sculptures, and other examples of sacred art from the early Middle Ages through the Baroque periods. Of particular interest is the portrait of Duke Rudolf IV: presumably painted in about 1360 in the court workshop of Prague, it depicts one of the most important of the Cathedral's patrons; it is believed to be the earliest portrait of the Duke and shows him in three-quarters profile, a departure from the traditional full-profile figure. Also of great importance are the altarpiece from Antwerp, sculpted in about 1450, and the Ober-St. Veit altarpiece, the Crucifixion of which is considered to be the most important German pictorial work of the early 16th century. It is by Dürer's pupil Hans Schäufelein. Almost across from the "Steffl," with its entrance at No. 7 in nearby Singerstrasse, we find the **Kirche**

Saint Rochus *(ca. 1500), the* Erlach Madonna *(ca. 1325) and the* Lament of Christ *in the Cathedral and Diocesan Museum.*

und Schatzkammer des Deutschen Ordens (Church and Treasury of the Teutonic Order). Consecrated in 1375, the church is one of the few Gothic buildings in which the transformations in Baroque style, with its characteristic oval elements, create a harmonious Gothic-Baroque composition.

The noteworthy *Flügelaltar* (Triptych), a 16th-century Dutch work, was in Danzig's Marienkirche until 1864. The **Schatzkammer** is also worth a visit: here are exhibited precious tableware and household furnishings from the 17th and 18th centuries as well as insignia, coins, ceremonial costumes, and arms.

GRABEN

The Graben, together with Kärntner Strasse and the Kohlmarkt, is the elegant shopping district of Vienna, a street for first-class purchases, a classical site for rendez-vous and meetings.

The unusual form of the Graben is striking: a large, elongated square in the pedestrian zone. About 300 meters in length and over 30 wide, the square lies over the moat of the ancient Roman *castrum*, which was filled in during the late 12th century and transformed into a wide street. At the time of Maria Theresa it became the famous meeting-place of the Vienna that counted and the no less famous center of high-class prostitution ("Grabennymphen"). At the center of the square rises the Baroque **Pestsäule** (Plague Column), commissioned by Emperor Leopold I in thanks for the end of the Plague of 1679 and erected by Johann Bernard Fischer von Erlach and Ludovico Ottavio Burnacini with the collaboration of other important artists of the time.

The two ends of the Graben are adorned by 19th-century fountains. Also of note are a number of buildings from

View of the Graben with the Plague Column. Below, detail of the Plague Column.

The Peterskirche in an engraving by Carl Schütz (1779).

The Baroque Peterskirche (Saint Peter's Church).

The interior of the Peterskirche.

the same century, such as the Biedermeier-style **Erste Österreichische Sparkasse** (First Austrian Savings Bank) at No. 21 and the Jugendstil buildings at Nos. 10, 14-15 and 16. The façade of the latter is decorated with floral motifs in colored majolica. To the right of the Graben as we come from the Cathedral is Petersplatz, on which the **Peterskirche** (Saint Peter's Church) is located. The Baroque church was built, with the collaboration of J. Lukas von Hildebrandt, in 1702-1715 on the site of an ancient church which according to legend was built by order of Charlemagne. The **interior**, with frescoes and ochre-and-gold stuccowork, is the work of famous Baroque artists including M. Altomonte, L. Mattielli, M. Steindl, S. Bussi, and A. Camesina. The *fresco of the dome* is a masterpiece by J. M. Rottmayr.

AM HOF

The beautiful, ancient, and elegant Naglergasse, also pedestrianized, leads from the Graben to the medieval city center and to the large square called Am Hof: trapezoidal in form, center of city political life through the centuries, it is still today one of the city's most significant sites. It was here that in the 12th century the Babenbergs built their Residence; in the past, tournaments and festivals were organized in this square delimited by beautiful homes and a church. At the center rises the **Mariensäule** (Column of Our Lady), promised to the Madonna by Emperor Ferdinand III in his prayers during the war against the Swedes and erected between 1664 and 1667 in place of a 1647 column. The triumphant Mary Immaculate tramples the serpent of the Apocalypse, while on the base armed angels battle four dragons, symbols of the four great scourges of mankind: war, famine, plague, and heresy.

The **Kirche "Am Hof,"** or Church of the Nine Choirs of Angels, built by the Carmelite friars in about 1400, was restored in 1607-1610 in Baroque style in the interior following a fire. The sumptuous façade of 1662, a beautiful example of early Baroque, was redesigned by the Italian architect C. A. Carlone.

The walls, side chapels, and dome in the **interior**, Gothic in

The Kirche "Am Hof." Above, the Mariensäule (Column of Our Lady).

The Zeughaus, once the city arsenal.

style with two aisles and a nave, are decorated with frescoes and stuccowork. On the high altar is a large altarpiece by J. G. Däringer, *Maria and the Choir of Angels*. In 1782, Pope Pius VI blessed the Viennese from the balcony of the façade, and on 6 August 1806, from the same spot, Emperor Franz II renounced the crown of the Holy Roman Empire when this secular political institution came to an end under pressure from Napoleon's forces.

It was in the **Palais Collalto**, at No. 13 next door to the church, that in 1762 Wolfgang Amadeus Mozart held his first concert in Vienna. In a corner of the square, in what was formerly the **Bürgerliches Zeughaus** (City Arsenal), a 16th-century building with statues by Lorenzo Mattielli on the façade, are the head-quarters of the Fire Brigade.

In one of the narrow old streets behind the "Am Hof" church, at No. 2 of the Schulhof, is the **Uhrenmuseum** (Clock Museum): it is one of the most interesting of its kind and a gem among the city's museums. The three floors of the small, old building exhibit over 3000 timepieces, some of which are true master-pieces of mechanics. Of note for their sheer richness are those with inlays in ivory, enamel, silver, and precious stones; and for its oddity a time-piece of rural origin with a pendulum in the form of a cow's tail. From the astronomical clock, the hands of which take 20,904 years to make one complete revolution, to the most precious of pocket watches: there is something for everyone.

FREYUNG

*A short street links the "Am Hof" square and the Freyung, another suggestive square of old Vienna. Of irregular form and encircled by beautiful palaces and the Scottish Church, its name (from frei,"free") dates back to the Middle Ages, when the Scottish Convent offered sanctuary to the persecuted; the poor reputation that accompanied the area for centuries may also date to the same period. The square also offers other artistic attractions: at No. 3 **Palais Harrach**, built in 1690 to plans by Domenico Martinelli; at No. 4 **Palais Daun-Kinsky**, one of the most beautiful Baroque buildings in Vienna, built in the years 1713-1716 by J. Lukas von Hildebrandt, with a great staircase of par-*

*The Austria-Brunnen.
Bottom, Palais Daun-Kinsky
and a detail of the portal.*

ticular interest in the interior; at No. 7 the **"Schubladkastenhaus"** (Chest of Drawers House), a strange name for the 16th-century Priory of the Scottish Convent—but as to form it does resemble a dresser. The square is also home to the **Austria-Brunnen** (Austria Fountain) designed by Ludwig Schwanthaler; this symbolic representation of Austria and the four great rivers of the Hapsburg Empire (Po, Vistula, Elbe, and Danube) was built in 1846.

The Benedictine church known as the Schottenkirche or Scottish Church. Below, the façade of the church and a detail of the bell tower.

Schottenkirche - The origins of the Scottish Church date back to the 12th century, when Duke Heinrich II Jasomirgott, the first of the Babenbergs to reside in Vienna, called in the Irish Benedictine monks from Ratisbona and donated large sums to their order. The monks, who during the Middle Ages were always erroneously called *Schotten* (Scotch), built the first Romanesque church. It was damaged many times over the following centuries by fires and collapses and was rebuilt in Gothic style following the earthquake of 1443. The Gothic altar had 24 important paintings by Scottish masters, 19 of which are on display in the convent gallery. Today's Baroque aspect dates to the years 1643-1648 and is the work of the Italian architects Andrea Felice d'Allio and Silvestro Carlone; the latest alterations date to the 19th century. Two heavy, low towers embellish the linear façade. In the **interior** are the two highly valuable Baroque side altars, the *Deckengemälde* (ceiling paintings) of the

The interior of the Scottish Church.

nave, executed by Julius Schmid in 1887-1889, and the *high altar*, work of H. Ferstel (1883). To the left is the entrance to the *crypt,* the burial place of Duke Heinrich II Jasomirgott. On the left side altar stands the most ancient statue of the Virgin Mary in all Vienna, dating to about 1250; it is said that the statue saved the city from the Swedish seige near the end of the Thirty Years' War.

Freyung-Passage - Between the Freyung and Herrengasse is a hidden passage that must be considered a true "jewel." In the so-called Palais Ferstel, which in the mid-19th century was the headquarters of the Austro-Hungarian Bank, it had fallen into decay and only recently, following massive restoration work, has it regained its ancient splendor. Passages, courtyards, marble staircases of varied hues covered by glass vaults, and a small, gracious square with the **Brunnen der Donaunymphen** (Fountain of the Danube Water-Sprites) are the ideal setting for a pleasant shopping trip to the modern, elegant shops. The completely restored Café Central, a meeting-place of intellectuals and writers during the last decades of the monarchy, invites you to stop for coffee and a sweet.

A portrait of the writer Peter Altenberg at the Café Central.

Vienna's Coffee Houses

The coffee house is a true institution in Vienna. The first shops with the modern function of café opened in the 18th century. During the 1800's, in parallel with the cafés that opened in the center of Vienna, there also arose the so-called "popular cafés," called *Tschercherl*, in the outskirts. In the second half of the 19th century, the cafés became more and more important: they were the haunts of men of letters, artists, and businessmen; the best-known *Literatenkaffee* is Griensteidl, near the Imperial palace. Over time, the coffee houses separated into various types, in part on the basis of their clientele. There are family cafés, billiard-players' cafés, cafés with gardens, cafés whose clientele is made up of artists and writers, theater cafés, and cafés with live music. Today, Vienna's cafés number about 2000.

History of the Viennese Coffee Houses

There are two versions of the story of how and when Vienna's cafés came into being. The first names 1685, when Emperor Leopold I granted a license to one Johannes Diodato to open a Turkish coffee bar. The second would set the date at 1683, when Vienna was besieged by the Turks. The legend narrates that when they retreated the Ottoman troops left behind 500 sacks of coffee. The city gave them to Joseph Georg Kolschitzky in thanks for his aid during the siege. Kolschitzky opened a shop selling coffee, the Zur blauen Flasche. In the beginning it seems that the Viennese disliked coffee prepared in the Turkish fashion; only when Kolschitzky began to filter it and add milk and honey, creating his "Mélange," did the populace begin to appreciate this drink.

The Café Central.
Below, the Silbernes Kaffeehaus
in a watercolor by F. Katzler.

Amalienburg, the
Leopoldinischertrakt
• p. 40/41

"In der Burg"
• p. 40

State
Apartments
• p. 38

Michaelerplatz
• p. 36

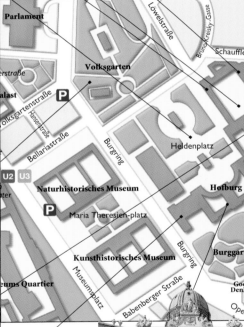

Parlament

Volksgarten

Schaufflergasse

Löwelstraße

Brunokreisky-Gasse

Heldenplatz

Hofburg

Naturhistorisches Museum

Maria Theresien-platz

Burggarten

Kunsthistorisches Museum

Burgring

Goethe
Denkmal

eums Quartier

Museumsplatz

Babenberger Straße

Opernring

U2 U3

Heldenplatz • p. 44

Volksgarten • p. 46

Spanish Riding School
• p. 50

Neue Burg,
the Neue
Hofburg
Museums
• p. 44/45

Hofburg • p. 37

Michaelerplatz - **Hofburg** - Michaelertrakt - **Kaiserappartements** (State Apartments) - **"In der Burg"** - Amalienburg - Leopoldinischer Trakt - Reichskanzleitrakt - Alte Burg - Burgkapelle (Imperial Chapel) - **Weltliche und Geistliche Schatzkammer** (Sacred and Secular Treasuries) - Heldenplatz - Neue Burg - Neue Hofburg Museums - Hofburg Gardens - Schmetterlingshaus (Butterfly House) - Stallburg - Josefsplatz - Nationalbibliothek (National Library) - **Spanische Hofreitschule** (Spanish Riding School) - Augustinerkirche (Augustinian Church) - Albertina

Michaelertrakt
• p. 38

Imperial
Treasuries • p. 43

Stallburg • p. 48

Josefsplatz, the
National Library
• p. 48/50

Alte Burg
• p. 42

Augustinerkirche
• p. 52

Imperial Chapel
• p. 42

Schmetterlinghaus
• p. 47

Albertina • p. 53

MICHAELERPLATZ

This beautiful, almost triangular square is the starting point for those who wish to visit "Imperial" Vienna. The statues and the fountains of the Michaelertrakt are but the prelude to the Imperial Residence, which was the hub of an empire with 50 million subjects. This square, with its many important monuments, merits much more than a passing glance.

Saint Michael's Church.
Below, view of the interior.

The **Michaelerkirche** (Saint Michael's Church) attracts attention immediately. This late Romanesque edifice, raised during the first half of the 13th century, was enlarged and transformed over the centuries that followed in the Gothic, Baroque, and classicized styles. The neoclassical façade by E. Koch (1793) is simple and unadorned; it is preceded by a Baroque porch by A. Beduzzi, dating to 1724-1725, topped by the sculptural group of the *Archangel Michael* by L. Mattielli. The soaring belltower (1598), with its many pinnacles, stands guard over the church. The interior has a nave and two aisles with transept and choir; above the high altar (1781), Vienna's last Baroque work, is a 16th-century *Byzantine icon* from Crete. The mortal remains of the poet Pietro Metastasio repose in the left transept; Karl Georg Mervill is the author of the main choir with the famous *Fall of the Angels*. Across from the church rises the sober and again unadorned façade of the Loos Haus, in evident contrast with the

richness of the architecture of the Imperial Palace. The **Loos Haus** takes its name from Adolf Loos, the important exponent of Viennese Jugendstil who built it in 1910. Its simplicity would represent a protest against what was called the "Ring Style" with its monumental forms and excessive ornamentation. Emperor Franz Joseph, who could not stand the sight of this bare building across from his windows, was outraged by its construction. The **Kohlmarkt**, the animated business street that leads to the Graben, opens off Michaelerplatz. Here you will find the famous Konditorei Demel, a classic among Viennese gastronomical addresses, at No. 11 in the Kohlmarkt.

The monumental entrance to the Hofburg in the Michaelertrakt (Saint Michael's Wing). Below, the two fountains at the ends of the building.

HOFBURG

For more than six centuries the Hofburg was the Residence of the Hapsburgs, who governed first as Emperors of the Holy Roman Empire and from 1806 onwards as Emperors of Austria. Frequent additions and transformations have made of it a complex embracing 18 buildings, 19 courtyards, 54 staircases, and 2600 rooms. The Hofburg has no intrinsic architectural unity; it is rather the legacy of a centuries-long history in which each epoch has left its mark: thus in a certain sense the complex represents a historical/artistic compendium of the Hapsburg monarchy. In these halls, stipulations of treaties of state and declarations of war alternated with merry balls; political intrigues and love stories, revolutions and fires, and six sieges made the Hofburg the main theater of Austrian history for many centuries. And still today, the Hofburg carries on an important function in the political life of the country: it is home to the offices of the federal President and an important international meeting center.

The old Burgtheater on Michaelerplatz, the most important theater of Vienna. Color engraving by Carl Postl, about 1800.

Michaelertrakt (Saint Michael's Wing) - Built between 1883 and 1893 where the Burgtheater once stood, to a partly-modified draft plan by the great architect Joseph Emanuel Fischer von Erlach, the Michaelertrakt became the main entrance to the Hofburg. Excavations in front of the entrance have revealed remains from Roman times, the Middle Ages, and the 18th century. A circular hall surmounted by a great dome leads from the Michaelerplatz to the inner courtyard, called **"In der Burg."** The façade is adorned with two fountains celebrating the power of the Hapsburgs over land and sea. The right fountain represents the *Dominion of Austria on Land* (1897), the left the *Dominion of Austria on the Seas* (1895).
The entrance to the State Apartments is to the left of the Michaelertor as we come from Michaelerplatz.

Kaiserappartements - Those of the State Apartments open to the public are all located in the wing housing the Reichskanzlei (Imperial Chancery) and the Amalienburg. An important visit this, one not to be missed, since wandering through the Emperor's rooms is certainly not something one can do every day. And it is a visit that will give us an idea of the difference between the simple lifestyle of Emperor Franz Joseph and that of his royal consort Elizabeth, who took care of her perfect body to the extreme with baths, beauty masks, and physical exercise. We can admire the refined Rococo furnishings or the exquisite Empire-style furniture and the splendid chandeliers in Bohemian crystal in the beautiful rooms that hosted Czar Alexander I during the Congress of Vienna (1815); further along is the banquet room with its table laid for dinner.

Imperial Apartments: the bedroom of Emperor Franz Joseph, the boudoir of Empress Elisabeth and the Imperial Banqueting Hall.

Our tour begins with the **Apartment of Archduke Stephan**, four rooms with valuable *Brussels tapestries* dating to the 17th century. Next is the **Apartment of Franz Joseph**, which includes among other attractions the Audience Chamber, with mural paintings by Peter Krafft, and the Conference Hall. The **Apartment of the Empress Elisabeth** is made up of six rooms; of particular interest are the bedroom and the bath (or dressing room) and the *statue of Elisa Bonaparte* by Antonio Canova (1817). The **Apartment of Alexander** contains 6 rooms featuring precious 18th-century Parisian wall-coverings; the **State Banqueting Hall** concludes the series of rooms open to the public. On one side of the entrance hall is the entrance to the **Hofsilber- und Tafelkammer** (Room of Tableware and Silver), where a

The courtyard known as "In der Burg"
with the monument to Emperor Franz I.

precious *collection of Chinese and Japanese porcelain* from the 18th century, a *Sèvres dinner service*, a vermilion dinner service for 140, a 33-meter long 19th-century bronze center-piece, and other court tableware are displayed. Your ticket also lets you visit the **Sissi Museum**, opened in 2004. Six rooms trace the life of the Empress Elisabeth from her childhood in Bavaria to her death at the hand of an assassin in 1898. Many personal belongings and famous portraits reveal the Empress' complex personality and facets of her private life: her wont to escape from the pomp of the court, her care of her face and body, her love for poetry.

"In der Burg" - As we exit the Michaelertrakt rotunda we come to this broad inner yard built in 1545 for Archduke Maximilian as a tournament ground. If the Schweizerhof can be said to represent the Gothic Hofburg and the Heldenplatz to embody the spirit of the 19th century, in the "In der Burg" square the Baroque has left clear and lasting marks. It was originally used for celebrations and tournaments (worth mention, above all, the famous ballet of horses given on the occasion of the wedding of Leopold I to Margherita of Spain in 1666), but it was also the theater of dramatic events such as the execution of officials and soldiers during the Turkish Wars. At the center of the yard is the *monument to Emperor Franz I,* who died in 1835. The sumptuous Schweizertor (Swiss Portal) leads in to the Schweizerhof.

Amalienburg - This wing of the castle, commissioned by Emperor Rudolf II, was erected between 1575 and 1611. The interior was completely renovated during the reign of Maria Theresa. Of note the **Turm** (Tower) added by Nikolaus Pacassi in 1764; the *lunar clock* that marks the phases of the moon is the work of

Tycho Brahe, well-known astronomer at the court of Rudolf II. The name of the building derives from that of Empress Amalia, widow of Joseph I, who lived here from 1711 until her death in 1742.

Leopoldinischertrakt (Leopoldine Wing) - Begun by Emperor Ferdinand I in 1547, construction of this wing of the Hofburg, added to link the Schweizerhof and the Amalienburg, was continued during the years from 1660 through 1667 by Emperor Leopold I; destroyed by the fire of 1668, the wing was finally lived in by the Emperor in 1681. Baroque additions were introduced in the entire Imperial Residence following Austria's victory over the Turks. Empress Maria Theresa and

The Amalienburg tower with the lunar clock by Tycho Brahe.

her husband Franz Stephan of Lorraine lived in this part of the palace, which is still furnished with the Empress' luxurious furniture. Since 1946, the wing has been the official residence of the federal President, whose attendance is signaled by the flying of the flag.

Reichskanzleitrakt (Imperial Chancery) - J. Lukas von Hildebrandt and Joseph Emanuel Fischer von Erlach began construction of this north wing of the Imperial Residence in 1723; it was

The Reichskanzleitrakt (Imperial Chancery).

The main entrance to the Reichskanzleitrakt, with the Labors of Hercules.

completed in 1730. The *Labors of Hercules* that decorate the main entrance are the work of Lorenzo Mattielli. The wing was the seat of government of the Holy Roman Empire until 1806.

Alte Burg - This fortified building, mentioned for the first time on 14 February 1279 in a document by King Rudolf I Hapsburg, was probably begun some years earlier (1275) by order of King Ottakar II of Bohemia. Of the original square-based construction with four massive corner keeps there remains only the **Schweizerhof** (Swiss Courtyard), which however underwent major transformation in the 16th century and so lost its medieval look. The name derives from the Swiss Guard, which garrisoned the castle during the time of Maria Theresa. The **Schweizertor** (Swiss Portal) is a sumptuous brick-colored Renaissance portal with gold inscriptions. It was erected in 1552 on the spot where the drawbridge stood in the 13th century.

The Renaissance Swiss Portal.

The Schweizerhof gives access to the **Burgkapelle** (Imperial Chapel). Perhaps the oldest part of the Hofburg, the construction dates to the years 1447-1449, when it was built by order of Friedrich III in place of an earlier chapel built for Duke Albrecht I (1296). Of considerable value are the late Gothic wooden sculptures,

The Schatzkammer (Imperial Treasuries): the crown of the Holy Roman Empire and the cloak of Emperor Franz I.

displayed on stands under canopies, representing the 14 Protector Saints and presumably made in the style of Niklas Gerhaert van Leyden, who also sculpted the funerary monument to Emperor Friedrich III in the Stephansdom.

On the tabernacle of the high altar is a small wooden crucifix. It seems that the Emperor Ferdinand II, sorely contrasted by the Protestant orders of Lower Austria in their fight for freedom of religion, heard Christ whisper from this crucifix: "Ferdinand, I shall not abandon you!" Since that time a copy of this cross is found in every Hapsburg chapel. It is in this chapel that the Wiener Sängerknaben (Vienna Boys' Choir) sings during Sunday morning Mass.

From the Schweizerhof we go on to one of the most famous and most valuable collections in the world: the **Weltliche und Geistliche Schatzkammer** (Sacred and Profane Treasuries), where hundreds of objects of inestimable value bear witness to the long and complex history of the Holy Roman Empire and its close ties with the Catholic Church. Twenty-one rooms are host to this collection of precious objects in gold, silver, and gems as well as exquisite embroideries and fabrics: the 10th-century *Imperial crown*, the 12th-century *Imperial globe*,

Vienna Boys' Chior

This choir was formed in 1498 by order of Maximilian I. Over its history, the choir was influenced by different styles, first Dutch and later Italian. Some famous musicians, like Joseph Haydn and Franz Schubert, were also members of the choir. With the fall of the monarchy, the choir fell on hard times: in 1920 it was disbanded, but was refounded in 1924. Today, it is supported by an association.

The choir's repertory ranges from medieval madrigals to contemporary works. The singers are divided among four choirs, each composed of 22-24 members. They perform every Sunday during Mass in the Burgkapelle and also give concerts at the palace concert hall and at the Opera. One group is often on world tour as Austria's ambassadors in music.

The sweeping Heldenplatz, with the Neue Burg.

On the right, the Äusseres Burgtor, the external gate opening onto the Ring.

the *silver sceptre*, the 12th-century Chinese silk *incoronation cloak* sewn in Palermo for King Roger II, the *Hapsburg Imperial crown* ("Hauskrone") dating to 1602, the *baptismal pitcher and bowl* used for Imperial family christenings, and the *silver cradle*, weighing a good 280 kilograms, given by the City of Paris to Napoleon I for his son, the King of Rome. A special place is reserved for the "Treasure of the Knights of the Golden Fleece," or the "Burgundian Inheritance," which with the wedding of Maximilian I to Mary of Burgundy became a Hapsburg possession; the Hapsburgs thus also inherited the title of "Dukes of Burgundy." Outstanding among the many highly valuable items in the collection is a masterpiece of medieval art, the 15th-century *Burgundian vestments*. The Sacred Treasury conserves liturgical ornaments and vestments and relics used and collected at Court. One of the most valuable pieces is the *reproduction of the "Am Hof" Mariensäule*, created in 1670-1680 by the goldsmith Philipp Kösel of Augsburg, who set it with over 3700 precious and semi-precious stones

Heldenplatz - From the "In der Burg" square, through a passage running under the Leopoldine Wing, we come to the vast Heldenplatz (Heroes' Square), once used for military reviews of the Imperial Army. The square is dominated by two great *equestrian statues*, one of *Grand Duke Karl* and the other of *Prince Eugene of Savoia*. The hemicycle of the Neue Burg opens at the end of the square; facing the Leopoldine Wing is the Äusseres Burgtor, and on its the right the square borders on the Volksgarten.

Neue Burg - This grandiose palace, completed in 1913, is the last construction bearing witness to Hapsburg power. It was

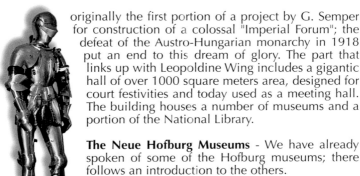

originally the first portion of a project by G. Semper for construction of a colossal "Imperial Forum"; the defeat of the Austro-Hungarian monarchy in 1918 put an end to this dream of glory. The part that links up with Leopoldine Wing includes a gigantic hall of over 1000 square meters area, designed for court festivities and today used as a meeting hall. The building houses a number of museums and a portion of the National Library.

The Neue Hofburg Museums - We have already spoken of some of the Hofburg museums; there follows an introduction to the others.

Ephesos-Museum - In the first years of the 20th century and again after the end of World War II, Austrian archaeologists were involved in excavations in Asia Minor and in particular in Ephesus in Turkey.

The finds from this region are displayed in this museum according to the most up-to-date exhibit criteria.

Worthy of attention here are the *colossal frieze* from the 2nd century AD, over 70 meters in length, commemorating the victory of Lucius Verus and Marcus Aurelius over the Parthians in 165 AD, and the *octagonal tomb* of a young woman and a part of the *sacrificial altar* of the great Temple of Artemides. The same entrance ticket also permits us to visit the **Waffensammlung** (Weapons Collection), containing historic armor and ceremonial weapons, and the **Sammlung alter Musikinstrumente** (Collection of Ancient Musical Instruments) with its Renaissance instruments (harpsichords, pianos, and many others) including the instruments used by the most illustrious of Austrian musicians (Brahms, Haydn, Schubert, Beethoven).

Ancient armor from the Weapons Collection at the Neue Hofburg.

The **Museum für Völkerkunde** (Ethnological Museum) houses objects from all parts of the world. Among these, on the ground floor, are the famous bronze statues from the Kingdom of Benin (an African kingdom the golden age whose dates from the 12th to the 18th centuries) and the celebrated *crown of feathers* and the *shield* given by the Aztec Emperor Montezuma to Fernando Cortez as a token of friendship. The first-floor exhibits include, among other things, handcrafted articles from Brazil, New Guinea, and Australia.

45

The Theseus-Tempel (Temple of Theseus).

Hofburg Gardens - Our visit to the Hofburg is certainly an extenuating one: halls, staircases, courtyards, and museums; a place to rest a while, suspending for a moment our walk, is a welcome relief. We therefore suggest a pause, and the Hofburg complex embraces not one but two parks that admirably serve the purpose: the **Volksgarten** (Public Garden) and the **Burggarten** (Castle Garden). The former is next to the Heldenplatz, in the direction of the Burgtheater; the other lies behind the Neue Burg. These two green oases, replete with fountains and statues, offer us the opportunity to relax in a natural setting of massive horse-chestnut trees and rose-beds. In the Volksgarten

The monument to Emperor Franz Joseph in the Burggarten.
The monument to Empress Elisabeth in the Volksgarten.

The monuments to Goethe and to Mozart in the Burggarten.

we find the *monument to Empress Elisabeth* ("Sissi"), where young couples habitually meet. In the Burggarten, instead, don't forget to stop at the *Mozart Memorial*, or to stroll along the shores of the lake, or to see the *monument to Emperor Franz Joseph* or the *Schmetterlinghaus* (Butterfly House). This one of the world's most beautiful greenhouses, in Jugendstil, offers the visitor all the enchantment of a tropical forest where thousands of butterflies of myriad different species live in freedom.

Different epochs and styles overlay each other

The Schmetterlinghaus (Butterfly House).

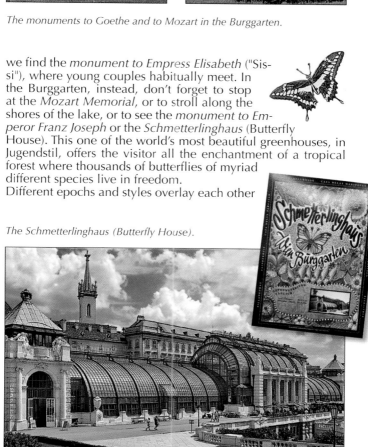

in the Hofburg complex, and while the effect as a whole is harmonious, it demands the visitor's undivided attention. Visiting the Hofburg is tantamount to making a journey through the centuries of Hapsburg dominion. Upon concluding our visit, we suggest returning through the "In der Burg" square and the Michaelertor to the Michaelerplatz, on the right of which we find still another interesting wing of the Hofburg.

Stallburg (Imperial Stables) - The inner courtyard is perhaps the

most beautiful Renaissance work in all of Vienna. Built between 1558 and 1565 by Ferdinand I for his son Maximilian II, it was originally separated from the Hofburg and consisted of a large square courtyard with colonnaded sides. It was later transformed to provide stables for the Emperor's horses, and is today the stable of the Spanish Riding School. The Stallburg also hosts the *Lipizzaner Museum* (Museum of the Lipizzan Horse), which is well worth a visit.

The inner courtyard of the Stallburg (Imperial Stables).

Josefsplatz - In this square, one of the most beautiful and harmonious in all Vienna, the 18th century has works of uniquely high artistic and architectural value. Surrounded by splendid buildings, the square was until 1565 the riding-ground of the Spanish Riding School; only under Emperor Joseph II did it take

The National Library seen from above.

The National Library.

on its present-day look. At the center of the square, an *equestrian statue* sculpted in 1795-1807 in a style recalling antiquity by Franz Anton Zauner, celebrates Joseph II.

Looking toward the National Library which runs down one entire side of the square, we see on the right the **Redoutensäle** (Redoute Rooms), dating to 1767 and formerly used as ballrooms and for theatrical events. On the left is a wing of the Augustinian convent, and across from the Library are the beautiful **Palais Pallavicini** (1784) and **Palais Palffy** (1575).

A detail of the statues on the National Library roof.

The Prunksaal, the gala hall of the National Library.

Nationalbibliothek - The building that houses the National Library is again linked to the names of the two greatest architects of the Baroque, Fischer von Erlach father and son; it was the latter who completed the building in 1735. The *Prunksaal* (Hall of Honor) is decorated with frescoes by Daniel Gran. The library owns about 7 million items, 2,500,000 of which are books, 300,000 manuscripts and incunabula, 183,000 papyri, 1,300,000 items in the theatrical collection, and 1,600,000 between the portrait collection and the iconographic archives. The rarest and most valuable specimens are on exhibit in the rooms open to the public.

Spanische Hofreitschule - White horses and proud riders in a setting of unequalled beauty and elegance: this is the Spanish Riding School. It has existed for over 400 years and is the greatest attraction in the Hofburg and indeed in all Vienna. In order to attend the performances you must make reservations many months in advance, but it is instead much easier to see the Lipizzaner horses at their morning training sessions, held every day except Sunday and Monday from February through June and from September through December. The queue to see this show, truly unique in the world, is worth every minute: the exercises performed with apparent ease and naturalness require years of training and a perfect concord between horse and rider that is extremely difficult to achieve. The Spanish Riding School was created in 1572 for military purposes. Originally, the hors-

The Lipizzan horses of the Spanish Riding School.

es were all Spanish and were destined for front-line combat alongside the regular cavalry. Today, the Lipizzaner are raised at the Piber Castle, near Graz. The school is housed in the **Winterreitschule** (Winter Riding School) built between 1729 and 1735 under the direction of J. E. Fischer von Erlach. The hub of the building is the hall, 55 meters in length, where the horses train and perform. This all-white hall is flooded with light and encircled by 46 columns that support the gallery. At the time of the Congress of Vienna, sensational celebrations were held here: for example, that on 2 October 1814, attended by 10,000 guests. The hall has also been the theatre of political events, such as the assembly of the citizenry during the 1848 Revolution. The Summer Riding School is located at the rear of the building.

Lipizzans

These members of an ancient breed created by the House of Hapsburg and the Austro-Hungarian monarchy are the horses used by the Spanish Riding School. Their name derives from Lippizza, near Trieste, where the horses were raised beginning in 1580. Lipizzans are white in color, extremely intelligent, and have a natural propensity for the classical gaits of the Haute École. Since the 18th century they have been appreciated not only as mounts for riding and dressage but also as coach horses. At the Spanish Riding School, the Lipizzans receive rigorous training in the paces (walk, trot, etc.) and the "airs" (various figures on and above the ground). Today, the Lipizzans are raised near the Austrian town of Piber.

The Augustinerkirche and a view of the interior.

From Josefsplatz, we continue down Augustinerstrasse to the last two stops on our itinerary: the Augustinian Church and the Albertina.

Augustinerkirche - The Court parish church, where Imperial weddings were held, was built in the 14th century in Gothic style. The interior was later remodelled in the Baroque style, but in 1784-1785 was again "Gothicized."

Interior - The Augustinerkirche is a high, narrow church with two aisles and a nave, all very simple in style. At the beginning of the right aisle we see the neoclassical *funerary monument to Archduchess Maria Christina* (favorite daughter of Maria Theresa) who died in 1798, by Antonio Canova (1798-1805). On the right, alongside the choir, is the two-aisled 14th-century **St. Georgskapelle** (Saint George's Chapel). The Augustinian Church, like others in Vienna, is a Hapsburg burial place. A niche in the Chapel houses the **Herzgruft**, where 54 silver urns

The funerary monument of Archduchess Maria Christina, by Antonio Canova.

The Albertina with the statue of Archduke Albrecht.
Below, detail of the Danube Fountain at the Albrechtsrampe.

each containing the heart of a member of the Imperial family are kept. The "oldest" heart is that of Ferdinand II (1578-1637), while the latest arrival is that of Archduke Franz Karl (1802-1878), father of Emperor Franz Joseph.

Albertina - The name derives from its founder, Duke Albert of Sachen-Teschen. The palace, enlarged in the years 1801-1804, houses one of the world's largest graphics collections (**Graphische Sammlung**), with about 60,000 drawings and more than one million prints. Among other items, the collection includes

works by Leonardo da Vinci, Raphael, Rubens, Rembrandt, Cranach, Bruegel and Dürer as well as by the modern artists Picasso, Matisse, and Chagall. Exhibits of certain sections of the collections open to the public are held periodically.

A staircase beginning at the museum entrance leads up to the panoramic terrace on which we find the *equestrian statue of Archduke Albrecht*; from here, on the right, another flight of stairs leads down to the Burggarten.

The Hare by Albrecht Dürer, in the Graphisches Sammlung.

53

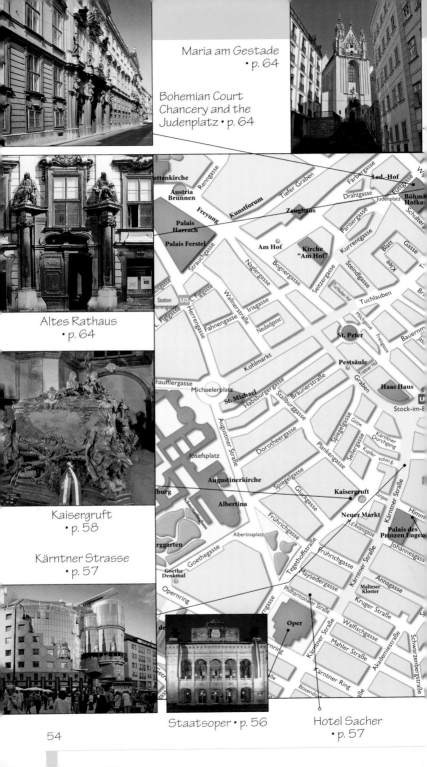

Maria am Gestade • p. 64

Bohemian Court Chancery and the Judenplatz • p. 64

Altes Rathaus • p. 64

Kaisergruft • p. 58

Kärntner Strasse • p. 57

Staatsoper • p. 56

Hotel Sacher • p. 57

Staatsoper - Hotel Sacher - **Kärntner Strasse** - **Kaisergruft** (Imperial Crypt) - Stadtpalais des Prinzen Eugen (Winter Palace of Prince Eugene) - Franziskanerkirche (Franciscan Church) - Mozarthaus (House of Mozart) - Dominikanerkirche (Dominican Church) - Schönlaterngasse - Heiligenkreuzerhof - Bernhardskapelle (Chapel of Saint Bernard) - Jesuitenkirche (Jesuit Church) - Akademie der Wissenschaften (Academy of Sciences) - Alte Universität - **Hoher Markt** - **Altes Rathaus** - Böhmische Hofkanzlei - Judenplatz - **Maria am Gestade** (Church of Saint Mary on the Bank) - Fleischmarkt - **Ruprechtskirche** (Church of Saint Ruprecht)

Hoher Markt
• p. 63

Church of Saint Ruprecht • p. 65

Heiligenkreuzerhof and Bernhardskapelle • p. 61

Mozarthaus • p. 59

Jesuit Church, Academy of Sciences • p. 62

Franciscan Church • p. 59

Winter Palace of Prince Eugene • p. 59

STAATSOPER

Haydn, Mozart, Beethoven, Schubert, Strauss, Mahler: these few names suffice to suggest the importance of Vienna in the history of world music. With the Scala of Milan and the Metropolitan of New York, the Vienna State Opera House is one of the most famous theaters in the world; here are held magnificent theatrical events as well as the famous Opera Ball that recreates for spectator the ancient splendor of the Imperial capital.

The Opera Ball

One of the symbols of Vienna is without doubt the Opera Ball, the society event at which young ladies of well-to-do families make their debut. The first Ball was held on 11 December 1877 and was called the "Hofopern-Soiree," a gala evening that was received enthusiastically by all the participants. The first true Opera Ball was held in 1935; the event was suspended during World War II and the first postwar Ball was organized for 2 February 1956. Every year, the Opera Ball represents a key moment in Carnival celebrations; it is held on the Thursday preceding Ash Wednesday and opens with an exhibition by the Opera House ballet. Another of Vienna's important society events is the Kaiserball, held at the Neue Burg on New Year's Eve.

The Viennese Waltz

Each year, the Opera Ball opens with a waltz danced by the young debutantes. The word "waltz" came into use in the late 1700's to indicate the conclusive figure of the Ländler, a south German folk dance. The waltz is danced by couples in 3/4 time. The term "Viennese waltz" appeared for the first time in 1811 at Braunschweig, and the dance reached the height of its splendor with Johann Strauss father and son. Among the most famous waltzes composed by these two musicians are *An der schönen blauen Donau* ("Blue Danube") and *Die Schwalben*.

Construction work on the Staatsoper, completed in 1869, was the subject of violent debate which eventually caused the deaths of the architects who had designed it, E. van der Nüll and A. von Siccardsburg: one committed suicide and the other died of a heart attack two months later. Neither was able to attend the inaugural performance of Mozart's *Don Giovanni* in 1869.

In 1945, the Opera was almost completely destroyed by bombing. It was rebuilt after the war to incorporate the most advanced technology of the time; today's auditorium boasts a seating capacity of 2209.

Guided tours give us an idea of the interior, with the splendid Grand Staircase and its *statues of the nine Muses* by Joseph Grasser, the beautiful frescoed lunettes of the foyer, and the boxes by Moritz von Schwind, miraculously intact despite the damage caused by the war. Outside, to the sides of the Opera building, are two graceful fountains. Behind the striking theater building is another well-known attraction of Vienna (especially for those with a sweet tooth): the **Hotel Sacher**. Always a venue for "the Vienna that counts," it was also theatre of political intrigues, secret meetings, and love stories of European-scale resonance. The name naturally evokes the famous *Sachertorte*, a specialty of Viennese cuisine.

KÄRNTNER STRASSE

This wide street linking the Ring with Saint Stephan's Square is part, together with the Graben, of the pedestrian area and may be considered the elegant "promenade" of Vienna. The benches under the horse chestnut trees beckon us, promising a relaxing pause and, in summer, the tables of the many cafés and restaurants are very pleasant stopping and meeting places. Young musicians offer a romantic parenthesis for those who stroll down this street at leisure. Lining the route are luxury boutiques and famous cafés (like Sirk, at No. 53, across from the Opera), a tradition that has become a part of Viennese culture. On the right in the first stretch is the **Malteserkirche**, a small Gothic jewel, dating perhaps to the 14th century; behind its neoclassical façade it contains memorabilia of the medieval Order of the Knights of Malta.

A short street at about the level of this church leads to the *Neuer Markt*. Near the Malteserkirche we find the **House of Music**, which invites the visitor to undertake a journey on which music is perceived as a harmonious fusion of hearing and sight. The *Philharmonic Museum*, on the first floor, presents the history of this world-famous orchestra. The third floor pays homage tro Austria's greatest musicians (Haydn, Mozart, Schubert,

Facing page, the Staatsoper.
The Haashaus on the
Stephansplatz.

57

Strauss, Mahler, Schönberg, Berg) in their "natural habitat," with documents, models, costumes, and original scores. At the point in which Kärntner Strasse runs into Saint Stephan's Square there stands the trunk of an old tree, called the **"Stock im Eisen,"** in which every craftsman who left the city in olden times was wont to plant a nail to ensure that he would return. Facing the Stephansdom is the **Haashaus** with its surprising asymmetrical façade. This building is the work of the famous Austrian architect Hans Hollein, who completed it in 1990.

KAISERGRUFT

The **Neuer Markt** (New Market) square is home to the **Kapuzinerkirche** (Capuchin Church), a small Baroque building erected in the years from 1622 to 1632 and selected by the Hapsburgs for celebrating the funeral ceremonies for members of the Imperial family. To the side of the façade is the passage to the Kaisergruft, the imposing Hapsburg Crypt, where since 1633 all the members of the family (144), including 12 emperors and 16 empresses, have been entombed. To the right of the entrance, beginning from the Gründergruft (Crypt of the Founders), we immediately come upon the burial place of Emperor Matthias and his wife Anna of Tyrol, then those of Ferdinand III, Leopold I, and Joseph I. From this ancient crypt we go on to the room in which Maria Theresa and her husband Franz Stephan lie in a double Rococo tomb, the most beautiful in the Imperial crypt, by B. F. Moll. The last four rooms are the final resting places of Emperors Leopold II, Franz II, Ferdinand I of Austria, and Maximilian of Mexico. In the last crypt, facing the chapel before the exit, are the tombs of Franz Joseph, sovereign of the Austro-Hungarian Empire for 68 years, and those of his consort Elizabeth ("Sissi") and their son Rudolf, who both died in tragic circumstances.

*Above, the Kapuzinerkirche.
The funerary monument to Maria Theresa and her husband in the Kaisergruft (Imperial Founders Crypt).*

Following our visit to the Kaiser-gruft, we proceed down Donner-gasse, cross Kärntner Strasse and continue on Himmelpfortgasse, where at No. 8 stands the **Stadt-palais des Prinzen Eugen** (Winter Palace of Prince Eugene), a Baroque masterpiece raised at the turn of the 18th century. Built by Fischer von Erlach the Elder and J. Lukas von Hildebrandt, the palace is today the seat of the Ministry of Finance. Very close by, at No. 6, is the Café Frauenhuber, founded by Maria Theresa's personal chef and patron-ized by Mozart and Beethoven.

The Franciscan Church.

FRANZISKANERKIRCHE

The Franciscan Church was built between 1603 and 1611 on the site of an earlier Franciscan convent: originally in Renais-sance style, it was altered in the 18th century. The **interior** has a single nave and contains works by famous Baroque artists: the dramatic, phantasmagorical *high altar* (1707) is by Andrea Pozzo, while the artistically-carved *organ* (1642) in the choir behind it is by J. Wöckert. At the center of the church square stands the *Mosesbrunnen* (Moses Fountain), a work by Johann E. Fischer dating to 1798.

From Franziskanerplatz, we cross Singerstrasse and proceed down Grünanger-gasse to Domgasse. The block marked out by these streets and by the Blutgasse offers us one of the most outstanding examples of slum clearance in Vienna. Where until only a few years ago were reeking alleys and old houses there now rises a modern building complex with gardens, art galleries, shops, and *Kaffeehäusern* (multi-storied cof-fee shops where one may stop for a while, read the newspapers, and receive guests). At No. 5 Domgasse is the so-called **Mozarthaus** (House of Mozart), where Mozart lived from 1784 through 1787 during his most creative period. It was here, as we are reminded by the plaque on the Schulerstrasse side, that he com-posed *The Marriage of Figaro* as well as other masterpieces. Today, the apartment has been transformed into a museum which preserves many objects that remind us of the great musician. Only a few steps

The Mozarthaus.

Wolfgang Amadeus Mozart

Wolfgang Amadeus Mozart represents one of the vertexes of the history of world music. His musical production gives form to the technical, compositive, and expressive conquests of the 18th century: from the Baroque and Rococo to Classicism and early Romanticism. Mozart was born in Salzburg in 1756; at age six, he visited Vienna for the first time with his family and played for Empress Maria Theresa. In 1779 he was engaged as court organist in Salzburg, where he remained until 1781 when he left his native city for Vienna. In the capital, he met his wife, Costanze Weber, and composed several of his most famous works: *The Marriage of Figaro, Così Fan' Tutte,* and *The Magic Flute.* In 1787 he was named court chamber musician. Mozart died suddenly on 5 December 1791.

Mozartkugeln

These famous chocolates were invented in 1890 by the Salzburger Paul Fürst. At first, the confectioner called them "Mozartbonbon" and only later by the name by which they are known world-wide today: Mozartkugeln. Paul Fürst received a gold medal in Paris for his invention. The chocolate-covered Mozartkugeln have a center of marzipan mixed with pistachio nuts.

away is the Wollzeile, a long business street with many bookshops. At No. 5, in a passage leading through closed-in courtyards to Saint Stephan's Square, is "Figlmüller," one of the most characteristic eating-places in Vienna.

At the level of No. 35 Wollzeile we turn into Postgasse, where we find the Baroque **Dominikanerkirche** (Dominican Church), built in the 17th century by J. Spatz, C. Biasino, and A. Canevale on the site of an older church. Schönlaterngasse begins alongside the church.

Schönlaterngasse - Along this beautiful winding street we find

many hospitable cafés and beer-houses and some true jewels of the art of ancient Vienna. No. 7 is the famous **Basiliskenhaus**, one of the oldest middle-class houses in the city; while dating to 1212, the building was much remodelled in the 16th and 17th centuries. Its name derives from a legend according to which a basilisk was found in a well by the house; it would seem that a baker had the brilliant idea of killing it with a mirror–and in fact, upon seeing its ugliness, the monster exploded. A figure of the basilisk decorates the façade of the house. At No. 6 we note the **Schöne Laterne** (Pretty Lantern), forged in 1680, from which the street takes its name.

The Schöne Laterne.

HEILIGENKREUZERHOF

The entrance to this immense courtyard, surrounded by beautiful 17th and 18th-century buildings, is at No. 5 Schönlaterngasse. For over 700 years it has been property of the monks of the Heiligen-kreuz (Monastery of the Holy Cross, near Mayerling in Wienerwald). Originally a city holding of the monastery, it was later transformed into a residential complex. The medieval look of the complex has been all but obliterated, above all by the 17th- and 18th-century al-terations which are responsible for its present-day look. Each of the buildings facing onto the large courtyard contributes in its own man-ner to creating the relaxing atmosphere that invites us to stop for a while. Of particular note is the Baroque **Bernhardskapelle**, (Chapel of Saint Bernard), the current aspect of which dates to about 1730. The altarpiece of the high altar is by M. Altomonte, the sculptures by Giovanni Giuliani, and the architectural frescoes by A. Tassi.

*Top, the entrance and a detail of one of the Heiligenkreuzerhof buildings.
A view of the Heiligenkreuzerhof.*

Jesuit Church: a view of the interior and the trompe l'oeil *ceiling frescoes. Below, the façade.*

Not far from the Heiligenkreuzerhof, closed in by three buildings of considerable historic and artistic interest, we find the beautiful **Dr. Ignaz-Seipel-Platz**, one of the focal points of the 1848 Revolution, which today bears the name of a Chancellor of the First Republic.

The **Jesuitenkirche** (Jesuit Church), with its façade delimited by two bell-towers, dominates the square. Built during the Counter-Reformation, it owes its richly decorated interior to Andrea Pozzo (early 18th century). The *High Altar* and the *ceiling frescoes* that create the *trompe l'oeil* effect of a cupola ("Scheinarchitektur") are well worth seeing.

To the right of the church stands the **Akademie der Wissenschaften** (Academy of Sciences), a Rococo building by N. Jadot raised by order of Maria Theresa in the years 1753-1755. The façade, decorated with columns, statues and a large balcony, is also embellished with two exquisite fountains on the walls to the sides of the main entrance. In the interior, it is worthwhile visiting the beautiful *Aula Magna*, with frescoes by Gregorio Guglielmi; unfortunately, what we see are copies, since the originals were destroyed in the fire of 1961. The facing building is the **Alte Universität**, a 14th-century edifice restructured during the 17th century for the Jesuits who then directed the University.

From Dr. Ignaz-Seipel-Platz we turn into **Bäckerstrasse**, with its many interesting buildings: at No. 7, a 16th-century Renaissance home with a lovely porticoed courtyard; at No. 8 and No. 16, two Baroque homes dating to the first half of the 18th century which display incontrovertible signs of the influence of the great architects of the age such as J. Lukas von Hildebrandt.

After having crossed a small square called **Lugeck**, at the center of which rises the monument to Gutenberg, we cross Rotenturmstrasse to the Hoher Markt.

HOHER MARKT

We may choose to visit the Roman ruins under the Hoher Markt, where we find the remains of homes of Roman officials dating to 100-300 AD along the main road that ran from east to west through the legionary *castrum*. Not far away, to the north, is the *praetorium*, headquarters of the Roman commander-in-chief. The Hoher Markt, devastated by bombing during World War II, has lost much of its fascination due to modern reconstruction. At its center is the Baroque **Vermählungsbrunnen** (Nuptial Fountain), built to a design by J. E. Fischer von Erlach in 1729-1732. The fountain is surmounted by a bronze canopy supported by columns;

Hoher Markt:
the Vermählungsbrunnen
(Nuptial Fountain).

on the base are the figures of the high priest celebrating the marriage of Mary and Joseph, and around them scenes from the life of Mary.

The right corner of the square hosts an interesting and singular work in Viennese Jugendstil above an arch on Rotgasse: the **Ankeruhr** (Anker Clock) created by F. Matsch in 1913. A figure from Austrian history glides across its face every hour; the spectacle at noon, when all 12 figures emerge, is enthralling.

The Ankeruhr (Anker Clock).

ALTES RATHAUS

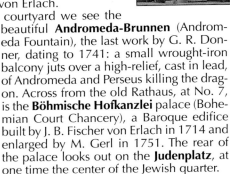

From the Hoher Markt, Wipplingerstrasse takes us to this ancient building at No. 8, the seat of city government since 1316. It was transformed repeatedly in the centuries that followed until in 1885 the city functions were transferred to the Neues Rathaus on the Ring. The Baroque façade, added between 1699 and 1706, shows the influence of J. B. Fischer von Erlach.

At the center of the courtyard we see the

beautiful **Andromeda-Brunnen** (Andromeda Fountain), the last work by G. R. Donner, dating to 1741: a small wrought-iron balcony juts over a high-relief, cast in lead, of Andromeda and Perseus killing the dragon. Across from the old Rathaus, at No. 7, is the **Böhmische Hofkanzlei** palace (Bohemian Court Chancery), a Baroque edifice built by J. B. Fischer von Erlach in 1714 and enlarged by M. Gerl in 1751. The rear of the palace looks out on the **Judenplatz**, at one time the center of the Jewish quarter.

The Altes Rathaus.
The Andromeda Fountain.

MARIA AM GESTADE

Proceeding along Wipplingerstrasse and then turning to the right, we come shortly to the small Church of Maria am Gestade (Saint Mary on the Bank). As its name suggests, the church was once on the bank of a secondary arm of the Danube. This church, mention of which dates to 1158, was destroyed by the fire of 1262 and rebuilt. The Romanesque church owes its present-day look to plans by the Grand Ducal master-builder Michael Knab: the choir dates to 1330-1369, the nave and the upper portion of the tower to 1398-1414. The steeple, with its light filigreed stone cupola, is the emblem of the church. In 1812 Emperor Franz I ordered restoration of the church after it had been used as stables and depot by Napoleon's troops.

Two splendidly painted panels of the original Gothic altar, dating to about 1460 and among the most beautiful of their time, hang at the two sides in front of the high altar, facing the visitor. To the right is the *Coronation of the Virgin* (with the *Crucifix-*

Church of Maria am Gestade.

ion of Christ on the back), to the left the *Annunciation* (with *Christ in the Olive Garden* on the back).

Other excellent examples of Gothic art include the figures on the columns, sheltered by the elegant canopies; of special interest those of the *Angel of the Annunciation* and *Maria*, dating to about 1370. The panes of various of the church's windows, most of which date to the 14th century, have been re-used in the choir and in the two windows of the south face of the nave. The high altar, in neo-Gothic style, was erected in 1845-1846.

Maria am Gestade: the panel-painting of the Annunciation *(ca. 1460) beside the high altar.*

A short walk along Salvatorgasse (running the length of the church and looking onto the rear of the old Rathaus) and then down Marc Aurelstrasse brings us to the oldest part of the city. Up a staircase and down narrow Sterngasse, we come to the **Fleischmarkt**, once the Greek business district. Today it is studded with inns and beer halls. The famous Griechenbeisl, at No. 11, is situated in a medieval home that since the 15th century has been the preferred inn of many celebrated personalities.

RUPRECHTSKIRCHE

From the Fleischmarkt, two short streets, Rabengasse and Seitenstettengasse (where the 18th-century Synagogue is located), lead to an elegant, secluded terrace on which is found the Ruprechtskirche (Church of Saint Ruprecht), one of the oldest in Vienna. Legend has it that the church was built by two disciples of Saint Ruprecht in the year 740. The nave and the lower portion of the bell tower date to the 12th century. The Gothic presbytery was built following the fire of 1276 and the Gothic aisle was completed in 1436. Above the church, the simple exterior of which is ivy-clad, rises a Romanesque bell tower with two lights windows. The two Gothic aisles of the **interior** house valuable works of art: the organ balustrade, dating to 1439 and, in the center window of the chancel, two precious stained-glass panes from the late 13th century showing the *Crucifixion* and the *Virgin Enthroned*. The new stained glass work is by Lydia Roppolt.

Church of Saint Ruprecht.

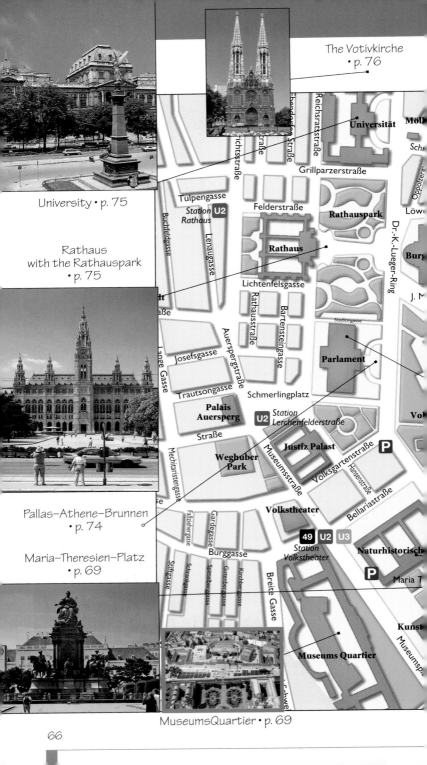

The Votivkirche • p. 76

University • p. 75

Rathaus with the Rathauspark • p. 75

Pallas–Athene–Brunnen • p. 74

Maria–Theresien–Platz • p. 69

MuseumsQuartier • p. 69

Map labels:

Universität
Möl
Sch
Ebendorfer Straße
Reichsratsstraße
...ichtsstraße
...traße
Grillparzerstraße
Oppolze
Tulpengasse
Felderstraße
Rathauspark
Löw
Station Rathaus U2
Buchfeldgasse
Lenaugasse
Rathaus
Dr.-K.-Lueger-Ring
Burg
...dt
Lichtenfelsgasse
...aße
Rathausstraße
Bartensteingasse
J. M
Stadiongasse
Lange Gasse
Auerspergstraße
Josefsgasse
Parlament
Trautsongasse
Schmerlingplatz
Palais Auersperg
Station U2 Lerchenfelderstraße
Vo
Straße
Mechtaristengasse
Weghuber Park
Museumstraße
Justiz Palast
Volksgartenstraße
Hansenstraße
P
Fassziehergasse
Gardegasse
Volkstheater
Bellariastraße
...e
Burggasse
49 U2 U3
Station Volkstheater
Naturhistorisch
Stiftgasse
Schrankgasse
Spitalberggasse
Gutenberggasse
Kirchberggasse
Breite Gasse
P
Maria T
Kunst
Museums Quartier
Museumsp...

MuseumsQuartier • p. 69

Ringstrasse - Äusseres Burgtor -
Maria-Theresien-Platz - **MuseumsQuartier**
(Museum Quarter) - **Kunsthistorisches Museum**
(Museum of the History of Art) -
Naturhistorisches Museum
(Museum of Natural History) - Parliament -
Pallas-Athene-Brunnen (Fountain of Athena Pallas)
- **Burgtheater** - **Rathaus** (City Hall) - Rathauspark
- Universität - Votivkirche - Minoritenplatz -
Minoritenkirche (Church of the Friars Minor)

Church of the
Friars Minor,
Minoritenplatz
• p. 77

Burgtheater • p. 74

The Ring, the
Äusseres
Burgtor • p. 68

Museum
of Natural
History • p. 72

Parliament • p. 74

Kunsthistorisches
Museum
• p. 70

67

RINGSTRASSE

About 5 kilometers long and ca. 60 meters wide, this sumptuous boulevard (*Ring*), together with the Donaukanal, encloses the historical center of Vienna; it is divided into various sections, each with a different name: Stubenring, Parkring, Schubertring, Kärtnerring, Opernring, Burgring, Dr. Karl-Renner-Ring, Dr. Karl-Lueger-Ring, and Schottenring.

In 1857, Emperor Franz Joseph ordered the demolition of the medieval walls that at the time still encircled the center of the city, and the ring road was built in place of the earlier bastions to serve that which was intended to become a capital city worthy of a great empire. The Ringstrasse, commonly called simply "the Ring," became the most important street in the city as soon as it was built. Along the grand artery were erected buildings for government and public administration, as well as noble residences and middle-class homes. A series of monumental works, squares, parks, monuments and gardens lend an extremely elegant cast to the whole. Despite the stylistic heterogeneity of its buildings, the Ring is lasting testimony to wealth and power. But it is an irony of fate that this grand boulevard, even while it was being built to symbolize the power and the grandeur of the Hapsburg Empire, was destined to witness its inevitable decline. It is still today a special experience to travel the Ringstrasse on foot or in a Fiaker and to relive the pomp and the splendor of the past. The monumental character of the buildings imitates on a grand scale the examples of Classical antiquity, of the Renaissance, and of the Gothic style: the State Opera House, the Kunsthistorisches Museum and the Naturhistorisches Museum, the Burgtheater and the Burgtor, the Parliament, the Rathaus, the University, the Votivkirche, and the Stock Exchange are the most important. And to these we must add the parks: the Stadtpark, the Burggarten, the Volksgarten, the Rathauspark, and many others.

The most attractive part of the Ring begins at the Opera. From the Burgring, we may go through the **Ausseres Burgtor** (also Heldentor - Heroes' Gate) to reach the Heldenplatz and the Hofburg. The triumphal portal was built in 1824 in place of the ancient fortifications destroyed during Napoleon's siege of 1809. In 1934, a monument to fallen soldiers was erected here.

MARIA-THERESIEN-PLATZ

This is one of the most striking points of the Ring: across from the Äusseres Burgtor, there opens out on the left the great square dedicated to Maria Theresa. Here, among flower-beds, lawns, and fountains, there rise one facing the other the two buildings of the Kunsthistorisches Museum and the Naturhistorisches Museum, with their high domes and beautiful

Monument to Empress Maria Theresa.

Neo-Renaissance façades decorated with columns and statues. The two museums were built between 1872 and 1881 by Gott-fried Semper and Karl Hasenauer with the aim of grouping to-gether the Imperial collections. In the interiors are halls frescoed by the most important artists of the age, such as Klimt, Makart, and Munkáczy. The great **Maria-Theresia-Denkmal**, completed in 1887 after 13 years of work, rises at the center of the square. At the feet of the Empress, whose enthroned figure reigns on the soaring monument, are represented the most important per-sonalities of the time: on horseback, her generals, and stand-ing, Kaunitz, Liechtenstein, Gluck, Haydn, Mozart, and others who contributed to the glory of her empire. West of the square is the **MuseumsQuartier** (Museum Quarter - see drawing on p. 128). The heart of the 60,000 square meter complex, one of the world's ten largest cultural districts with 50 different facilities for culture and modern and contemporary art, is the work of Fischer von Erlach father and son, built as an Imperial stables and mews between 1723 and 1725. The complex is characterized by mul-tiplicity: figurative and scenic arts intertwine with architecture, music, theater, the new media, and culture for children. There are exhibition spaces (Kunsthalle Wien and Architekturzentrum Wien) and niche cultural initiatives (Quartier21). The Museum-sQuartier is the home of important museums like the Leopold Museum and the Ludwig Foundation Museum of Modern Art.

Leopold Museum – This museum houses the formerly private collection of Rudolf Leopold. It includes 19th and 20th centu-ry works, above all masterpieces from fin-de-siècle Vienna by Klimt, Gerstl, Moser, Kokoschka, and Boeckl and world's most important Egon Schiele collection. The museum also exhibits fur-niture and tableware from 1900's Vienna by Otto Wagner, Adolf Loos, and Joseph Hoffmann.

Museum Moderner Kunst Stiftung Ludwig Wien (MUMOK) – The Ludwig Foundation's MUMOK is Austria's largest museum

An aerial view of the MuseumsQuartier.

of modern and contemporary art. The works on display link the most significant artistic movements of the 20th century: Realism, Formal Art, Fantastic Realism, Surrealism, Happening, Pop Art, Phototrealism, Abstract and Geometric Art, and Viennese Actionism. The MUMOK is home to the works of such famous artists as Klimt, Schiele, Kokoschka, Kandinsky, Mondrian, Picasso, Klee, Warhol, and many others.

KUNSTHISTORISCHES MUSEUM

The visitor interested in art history simply cannot miss the innumerable masterpieces contained in this museum. On three floors, its 91 rooms exhibit four great collections: Egyptian and Oriental art and art of the Classical Age, sculpture and the applied arts, the picture gallery, and the coin cabinet.

Mezzanine - Immediately to the right of the foyer are the **Ägyptisch-Orientalistische Sammlung** (Egyptian and Oriental Collection) and the **Antikensammlung** (Classical Collection), consisting of more than 4000 works of art, only a part of which is on exhibit. The Egyptian collection displays finds from the Pre-Dynastic era until Roman times. From the point of view of content it is divided into three parts: the cult of the dead (Rooms I, II, V), the history of Egyptian culture (Rooms II, IV, VI, VIa), and figurative art–in particular full-round sculpture (Rooms VII, VIII, IX). Don't miss the *tomb chamber of Prince Ka-Ni-Nisut* from Giza (ca. 2400 BC). There are also many objects from daily life: fabrics, tools, jewelry, etc. The most important works in the Oriental Collection are finds relating to the culture of ancient southern Arabia. The Classical Collection contains works dating from the 3rd century BC to 1000 AD, including Cypriot, Etruscan, Greek, and Roman sculptures and terracottas, like the Amazon sarcophagus and the copy of the *Youth from Magdalensberg*. The gem of the notable series of 1st- to 3rd-century AD Roman cameos is the famous 1st-century *Gemma Augustea*, representing the apotheosis of Emperor Augustus. Among the Byzantine, late medieval, and 5th-century gold Germanic items, pride of place goes to the *Treasure of Nagyszentmiklós*, also called Attila's Treasure, consisting of 23 golden vessels (9th-century pre-Bulgarian art) found in Hungary.

The façade of the Kunsthistorisches Museum.

In the left wing is the rich **Kunstkammer** (collection of sculpture and applied arts). The museum also owns a splendid collection of 800 French and Flemish (Gobelin) tapestries, which for reasons of conservation cannot be exhibited. The Kunstkammer collection includes Austrian Baroque and Rococo works, furniture, objects, and equestrian statuettes in ivory portraying three Hapsburg emperors and created by B. Steinle in 1662–1664; German, Dutch, and Italian Baroque items; 16th- and 17th-century vases in stone and precious metals and German goldsmithery; and bronzes and sculptures from the Italian Renaissance.

The beautiful Cup of St. Michael, in gold and precious stones (1530), is from France. There are also many important works by Italian artists: three bronzes by Giambologna, Benvenuto Cellini's gold *Salt Cellar* dated 1540, and sculptures by Desiderio da Settignano (*Laughing Boy*) and Francesco Laurana (*Bust of Isabella of Aragon*, late 15th century). Also of note are several medieval works, including the *Falconer* by Anton Pilgram, the *Madonna of Krumau*, and the *Allegory of the Transience of Earthly Things* (dated ca. 1500). The museum also boasts a section dedicated to clocks and the automata of the 16th century.

First Floor - This astonishing collection is made up of about 1600 paintings by German, Flemish, Dutch, Italian, Spanish, and French artists. Founded in the 17th century by Archduke Leopold Wilhelm, the picture gallery exhibits masterpieces of the Venetian Renaissance by Titian, Veronese, and Tintoretto, and of 15th- to 17th-century Flemish painting

Above on the left, Summer *by Arcimboldo (1563).*

Above, Madonna del Prato *by Raphael (ca. 1505).*

Jane Seymour Queen of England. *Portrait by Hans Holbein the Younger (1536).*

On the left, Peasant Dance *by Pieter Bruegel the Elder, 1568.*

71

with works by Rubens, (*Hélène Fourment*, the *Saint Idelfonso Altarpiece, Altarpieces of the Altar of the Jesuits*), Van Dyck (*The Fish Market*), and Van Eyck (*Cardinal Niccolò Albergati*). There are many works by painters of the Italian Renaissance and Baroque: Mantegna (*Saint Sebastian*), Parmigianino, Raffaello, Caravaggio (*Madonna of the Rosary, David with the Head of Goliath*), Reni, and Guercino. The Kunsthistorisches' Picture Gallery also boasts the largest assemblage of works by Pieter Bruegel the Elder, one of the most famous masters of Flemish painting (*Wedding Feast, Tower of Babel, Battle between Carnival and Lent, Hunters in the Snow, Children's Games, Calvary*). The collection of works by German artists like Dürer, Cranach the Elder, Cranach the Younger, and Holbein (portraits) is also very interesting.

Second Floor - Some of the rooms on this floor are occupied by the **Münzkabinett** (Coin Cabinet), a numismatic collection of great value containing examples from every historical era. Only about 2000 are displayed.

NATURHISTORISCHES MUSEUM

It was Franz Stephan I, husband of the Empress Maria Theresa, lover of the natural sciences and passionate collector, who laid the first stone of the minerals collection and procured many pieces which yet today form the nucleus of the Museum of Natural History collections. In 1889, Emperor Franz Joseph presided over the official inauguration of the museum, which in the meantime had been added to through acquisitions of the most disparate origins.

Today the museum, with its 39 exhibit rooms, is one of the largest and the most important of its kind. Its eight sectors (mineralogy/petrography, geology/paleontology, the prehistorical collections, anthropology, botany, and three zoology sections (on vertebrates, insects, and invertebrates) range over two floors.

Mezzanine - The collection, exhibited in 19th-century showcases in lavishly frescoed rooms, is a true source of wonder. Valuable minerals, stones of gigantic sizes, meteorites, fossils, and human skulls from 35,000 years ago alternate with many other interesting finds.

Rooms 1-5: A systematically-organized collection of minerals from all parts of the world, meteorites, and precious stones, among which a topaz weighing 117 kilograms, the largest *platinum nugget*

ever found (over 5 kg), a *salt obelisk* weighing 1680 kg, fragments of alexandrite of changing colors, and a specimen of the *lunar rock* brought to Earth in 1972 by the Apollo 17 astronauts; as well as diamonds of all kinds, gold nuggets, and crystals of Japanese stibnite. In Room 4, that of the precious stones, we can admire the *bouquet of gems* (2700 in all) given in 1760 by Maria Theresa to her husband Franz Stephan I, and several Colombian emeralds of absolute purity. Room 5 contains the meteorite collection. In **Rooms 6-10**, prehistoric flora and fauna illustrate the development of life on our planet during the Paleozoic, Mesozoic and Tertiary Eras. On exhibit in Room 6 are the oldest of the fossil plants; in Room 10, the impressive life-size reproductions of the enormous dinosaurs of the Mesozoic era (from 250 to 65 million years ago).

The **galleries near the staircase** house a large exhibit of finds from the Pleistocene glacial era (from 1,800,000 to 12,000 years ago), complete with exhaustive explanations of the causes and the spread of glaciation. Also on display are examples of European and American fauna.

Rooms 11-15: Collection of Stone Age finds, including the famous *Venus of Willendorf*, a small fertility figure in calcareous stone (20-30,000 years old).

Rooms 16-17: Anthropology section. The many exhibits chart the evolution of man over the last 35,000 years.

Room 18 is dedicated to children and was designed to provide young visitors with an initiation to the natural sciences: many of the objects, instead of being protected by glass, are exhibited in hands-on displays that invite small visitors to touch in order to learn.

First Floor - In the botanical and zoological sections are exhibited a great number of finds as well as anatomical specimens of animals of both existing and extinct species.

Room 21: Ecology, an exhibit centering on the fundamental laws of life on Earth.

Rooms 22-24 are dedicated to the invertebrates: there are thousands of mollusks, spiders, crustaceans, and insects.

Rooms 25-39 are instead those of the vertebrates: fish, birds, amphibians, reptiles, and mammals make up an immense, fantastic "inanimate" zoo. Among these, several species that are today threatened with extinction, including the Tasmanian wolf, the blue sheep, and the Carolina parakeet.

Facing page, Maria Theresa's bouquet of gemstones.
Above, a fossil frog of the Miocene era.
The Venus of Willendorf.

PARLIAMENT

We need not be expert connoisseurs of art to recognize the artistic and cultural influences that inspired the architect Theophil Hansen in the design of this work: they are very evidently those of ancient Greece. The imposing entrance and the tall columns that support the tympanum are striking in their sheer grandiosity. The building was completed in 1883 and until 1918 was the seat of the Council of State. Since the proclamation of the Republic it has been the seat of both branches of the legislature: the Nationalrat (National Council) and the Bundesrat (Federal Council). A double ramp, embellished with statues of Greek and Roman historians–among whom Thucydides, Herodotus, Tacitus, and Sallust–and by bronze sculptures of the Horse Tamers, leads to the entrance. In the square at the foot of the ramp stands the monumental **Pallas-Athene-Brunnen** (Fountain of Athena Pallas): the goddess of Wisdom, more than four meters tall, is surrounded by allegorical figures; in her right hand is Nike, the goddess of Victory.

The façade of the Parliament building with the Fountain of Athena Pallas. Detail of the interior decoration.

BURGTHEATER

Emperor Joseph II founded the Burgtheater in 1776 as the German National Theater. It was located in Michaelerplatz until 1888, year in which its home became the new building on the Ring constructed to plans by Gottfried Semper. The Burgtheater has always been one of the most important German-language prose stages. As is the case with many other important buildings in Vienna, the theater suffered heavy damage during the last war, but pains-

The Burgtheater.

taking restoration and enlargement work has restored it at least in part to its ancient splendor. On the side staircases, spared by the bombs, are some notable *paintings* by G. Klimt and F. Matsch. Of the many Viennese prose theaters, this is the most famous. During the season, which runs from September to June, at least 15 theaters are active in Vienna, offering a wide range of productions of both classical and modern works. To name just a few of the most well-known: the Akademietheater, the Theater in der Josefstadt, and the Volkstheater.

RATHAUS

The Neo-Gothic City Hall.

On the tower of the Neues Rathaus (City Hall), at 103 meters height, an iron horseman ("eiserner Rathaus-mann") armed with sword and banner stands guard over the fate of the city. Seat of the Mayor's offices and of the City Council, it is one of the most important Neo-Gothic buildings in Vienna. It was built between 1872 and 1883 by Friedrich von Schmidt. The façade of the building is distinguished by four side towers and the high center tower on which the *Rathausmann* stands: the statue, 3.4 meters tall and weighing almost 4 tons, is a work by the master ironsmith Alexander Nehr; not only is it the emblem of Vienna, but it also acts as a lightning rod! Many rooms in the interior are open to the public; for example, the Schmidt room, the City Council meeting room, which boasts a great bronze chandelier 10 meters in height and 254 lamps, and the great entertainment hall (Festsaal). One of the interior courtyards, the **Arkadenhof**, hosts the open-air concerts of the summer music festival. In front of the building, the shady, well-kept **Rathaus-park** looks out on the Ring. Under exotic trees, each supplied with a plaque with its name, among fountains and groups of benches, are many statues and monuments; one of these is dedicated to the kings of the waltz Johann Strauss the Elder and Josef Lanner. Along the boulevard that leads from the Rathaus to the Burgtheater are eight more statues of important figures in Austrian history.

UNIVERSITÄT

A short distance from the Rathauspark, on Dr. Karl-Lueger-Ring, there arises the massive University building in Neo-Renaissance style built by Heinrich von Ferstel in the years 1873-1883. The University of Vienna, founded in 1365 by Archduke Rudolf IV, is one of the oldest in central Europe. It was reorganized and enlarged during the illuminated rule of Maria Theresa, and since 1848, following the reform

implemented by the then Minister of Education Count Thun, has become a university with thousands of students who dedicate their time to their studies in monumental halls. Of particular note are the great Aula Magna and the beautiful arcaded courtyard, a true visual delight: a wide colonnade, decorated with the busts of illustrious professors who in the past taught in Vienna, surrounds 3000 square meters of lawns studded with trees; at the center is the **Kastaliabrunnen** (Kastalia Fountain) created in 1910 by E. Hellmer.

The University building and a view of the interior.

VOTIVKIRCHE

Like any reigning family, the Hapsburgs were the target of frequent assassination attempts. On this site, in 1853, the young Emperor Franz Joseph escaped death in an attempt on his life; his brother Maximilian, future Emperor of Mexico, ordered a church erected as a sign of thanks. Designed by Heinrich von Ferstel, who took his inspiration from the great French Gothic cathedrals of the 13th century, the Votivkirche was the first post-Baroque church in Vienna.

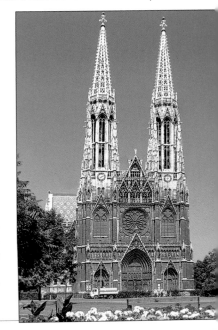

Two bell-towers, each 99 meters in height, rise at the sides of the façade, which is embellished by a sumptuous portal. The idea was that of building a temple celebrating illustrious Austrians, similar to London's Westminster Abbey, but the program was brought to fruit only in part: since 1945, the stained-glass windows of the left aisle have portrayed socially-committed personalities and in the chapel of the baptismal font only one of the planned funerary monuments, that of Niklas Salm, defender of Vienna during the first Turkish siege of 1529, has been erected.

The Votivkirche.

MINORITENPLATZ

If we go around the back of the Burgtheater in the direction of the Hofburg, we will come to Minoritenplatz (Minorite Square), a noble plaza in which an important part of city political life unwinds. At No. 3 we see the 17th-century **Palais Dietrichstein**, transformed in 1755 by L. F. Hillebrand, today seat of the Foreign Ministry. At No. 4 stands the **Stadtpalais Liechtenstein** (the winter residence of the noble family), with a beautiful side door by an unknown artist. Built to plans by Enrico Zuccalli and Domenico Martinelli in the years 1694-1706, the palace still belongs to the family. At No. 5, the **Palais Starhemberg**, today seat of the Ministry of Education and Sciences. Count Starhemberg, defender of Vienna during the Turkish siege of 1683, died here in 1701.

An Atlas at the side entrance to Palais Liechtenstein.

MINORITENKIRCHE

Begun in 1339, the Church of the Friars Minor was completed only at the end of the century. Badly damaged during the two Turkish sieges, the church was restored and transformed in Baroque style, but work in 1784-1789 by Ferdinand von Hohenberg restored all of its interior to the original Gothic style.
The church is set at the center of the square and has a high, sloping roof; on the façade is the important **Hauptportal** (Main Portal), work of the Parisian monk Jacob. The interior is divided by 8 columns into a nave and two aisles; in the left aisle is an exceptional mosaic, weighing 20 tons: a full-size reproduction of the *Last Supper* by Leonardo da Vinci, executed by Giacomo Raffaelli in the years 1806-1814.

The Minoritenkirche and its interior.

Gloriette • p. 83

Zoological Garden • p. 85

"Roman ruins" • p. 83

Fountain of Neptune • p. 84

Imperial Apartments: the Great Gallery • p. 82

Imperial Apartments: the bedroom of Franz Joseph and Elisabeth • p. 82

Schloss Schönbrunn (Schönbrunn Castle) - **Kaiserliche Appartements** (Imperial Apartments) - **Park** - Tiergarten (Zoological Garden) - Botanischer Garten (Botanical Garden) - Palmenhaus (Palm House) - **Wagenburg** (Imperial Coach Museum) - Technisches Museum (Technical Museum)

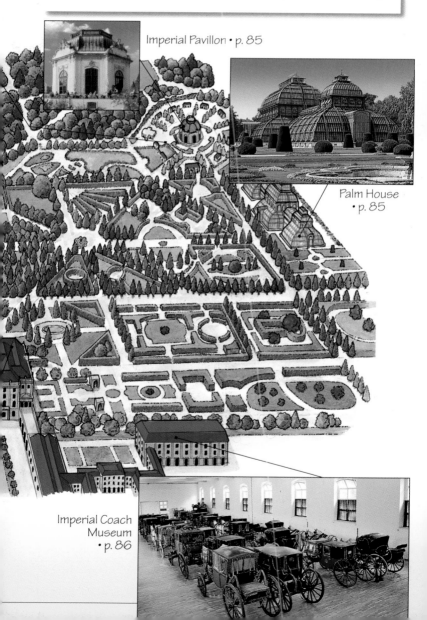

Imperial Pavillon • p. 85

Palm House • p. 85

Imperial Coach Museum • p. 86

SCHLOSS SCHÖNBRUNN

Schönbrunn is perhaps not the most beautiful of the Austrian castles, but it is undoubtedly the most famous. It can be reached from the center of Vienna, via underground, in just a few minutes. The station, a Jugendstil work by Otto Wagner, is right at the castle entrance, which is distinguished by two obelisks topped by the Imperial eagle.

A SHORT HISTORY OF THE CASTLE

Towards the middle of the 16th century, Emperor Maximilian II acquired a small hunting castle, the Katterburg, surrounded by extensive woodlands and fields; it was transformed by Maximilian himself and later by his successors. Unfortunately, the course of history was not clement to certain types of development: both the castle and the park were totally destroyed in 1683 by the Turks during the second siege of Vienna. Following the rout of the invaders, Emperor Leopold I charged the architect J. B. Fischer von Erlach with designing a grand castle just outside the city. The draft plan (1692/1693) surpassed all expectations: on the hill where today we see the Gloriette there was to have arisen a castle even larger than Versailles, the symbol of the powerful French monarchy and often object of envy by the Hapsburgs. But the wars had dried up the state treasuries, and Fischer von Erlach was forced to scale down his plans. In 1695 construction of the castle we see today was begun. Work dragged on for decades, until in 1743 Empress Maria Theresa employed Nikolaus Pacassi to complete the castle, adapting the original plans to the taste of the times. The Empress and her 16 children used Schönbrunn as their permanent residence and lent to the park and the castle itself their own personal

Schönbrunn Castle in a painting by Bernardo Bellotto (1759/60).

Schönbrunn Castle: the façade overlooking the garden.

touch. Joseph II, son of Maria Theresa, held little store in the pomp that had so attracted his mother and concentrated his interest mainly on the park. It was during his reign that the botanical garden and the zoological garden were inaugurated. During the centuries that followed, Schönbrunn bore witness to dramatic events: in the years 1805 and 1809 it was used as headquarters by Napoleon; and it was here that the capitulation of Austria was signed. From 1848 until the end of the long reign of Franz Joseph, the castle was used as the Imperial summer residence. On 11 November 1918, Karl I of Hapsburg signed his abdication here, so ending the centuries-long dominion of the Hapsburgs and paving the way to the Republic. And Schönbrunn has also been the venue for great international events even in more recent times: the historic East-West summit meeting between John F. Kennedy and Nikita Khrushchev, on 3 June 1961, is an example.

THE CASTLE

*As we near Schönbrunn, the castle appears as a wide, low construction of a color known as Schönbrunn yellow or Imperial yellow. A beautiful wrought-iron Rococo gate, with an obelisk at either side, opens into the grandiose **Ehrenhof** (Court of Honor), a large open area surrounded on three sides by buildings, where military reviews and open-air entertainments were held in the 18th century. On the right is the small but quite magnificent **Schlosstheater**, inaugurated in 1747 and modified in 1766-1767 by Ferdinand von Hohenberg, where summer performances are still held. Haydn directed here in 1777, Mozart in 1786.*
At the center of the linear façade, flanked by columns, is the entrance to the Imperial apartments and to the park.

Kaiserliche Appartements - Of the 1400 rooms in the castle, only 40 are accessible to the public. These rooms give us an idea of the style of life of the Hapsburgs and of the taste of the times: Maria Theresa's love for the exotic, Franz Joseph's sobriety, and

*The Imperial Apartments:
Franz Joseph's bedroom.*

the luxury of the public reception halls. The Rococo decorations characteristic of these interiors are by Nikolaus Pacassi. The two very beautiful majolica heating stoves were fired by the servants from the entrance so as not to disturb Their Highnesses.

Our visit to the apartments begins with the 10 rooms of the **apartment of Franz Joseph**: the Emperor was famous for his Spartan lifestyle and his refusal to accept innovation. It is even said that he protested the installation of electric power in the castle. His extremely sober personality is also mirrored in the furnishings: the camp-bed we see here is that in which he died on 21 November 1916. In striking contrast, the public reception halls and the **apartment of Maria Theresa**, where luxury and pomp unite to create an unequalled impression of richness, are the overt expression of a great woman and a powerful empire. Tapestries, porcelains, chandeliers, and rare pieces of Chinese and Japanese art and furnishings in valuable woods fill these rooms. Worth special attention are the **Hall of Mirrors**, where Mozart, still a child, gave a concert for Maria Theresa; the **Vieux-Laque-Zimmer**, the walls of which are decorated with exquisite oriental lacquered panels that were painted on the high sea to avoid dust marring the surfaces; the **Chinese Rooms**, often used for secret political meetings and private discussions, with precious *Ming porcelains*; the **Porcelain Room**, the wooden panelling of which creates the effect of porcelain; the **Milionen-Zimmer**, called thus due to the high cost

The Imperial Apartments: the Great Gallery.

The Gloriette.
Bottom, the entrance to one of the side wings of the Gloriette.

of its decoration in precious wood (ficatin) brought from Guiana and the Antilles, and to the precious 16th-century *Indian and Persian miniatures* it houses; the **Great Gallery**, 43 meters in length, which was used for banquets, court entertainments and important meetings.

To the left of the entrance are the **Bergl-Zimmer**, frescoed with floral motifs, figures of animals, and tropical plants by Johann Bergl in 1769-1777. The rooms, open from May through September, were the favorite retreat of Maria Theresa during the heat of summer; Crown Prince Rudolf later lived here.

Park - The **Schlosspark** has an even more grandiose aspect than the castle: with its oft-restructured 1.6 square kilometers, covering almost the same area as Vienna's first Bezirk (Innere Stadt), it loses nothing by comparison with French models. It is the ideal setting for a relaxing stroll after our visit to the Castle rooms. As we walk slowly down the shady lanes, among high espalier hedges that conceal fountains and Roman ruins, it is easy to become enchanted with the romantic atmosphere; Baroque pavilions and statues follow one another over the lawns and under the trees, from which playful squirrels look out in the hope of scrounging nuts from visitors.

Upon entering the park, our attention is drawn by the **Glori-**

Detail of the Fountain of Neptune.

ette, the elegant neoclassical arcade that dominates the low hill south of the castle. It was built, together with many other parts of the park, by Ferdinand von Hohenberg in 1775 in remembrance of the Austrian victory over the Prussians in 1757 at Kolin. The Gloriette, 19 meters in height and 95 meters wide, decorated with trophies, animal skulls, and armor, is the best vantage point for enjoying the panorama of the castle and the park, as it offers a view that sweeps over the entire city. And so it is imperative to climb the gently-sloping hill and to linger near the elegant flower-beds that are re-planted three times a year (in spring, they all boast Dutch tulips). Below the great flower-beds, at the foot of the hill, is the monumental **Neptunbrunnen** (Fountain

Fountains in the castle park.

of Neptune), dating to 1780, a worthy cap to the lower park. From the Gloriette, to the right facing the castle, a path through a wooded area leads us to imitation Roman ruins and to the **Schöner Brunnen**, the "beautiful fountain" from which both the castle and the park took their names. Returning to the avenue along the flower-beds, we reach the entrance to the **Schönbrunn Zoological Gardens**, built in 1752 by Franz Stephan of Lorraine, consort of Maria Theresa, and later expanded by their son Joseph II: this is the

The Palmenhaus.

world's only example of a Baroque zoo. The original structure had become the object of continual repairs; over the last few years a goodly portion of the zoo has been renovated according to contemporary criteria in order to provide better living conditions for its thousands of animal guests. Not far away is another jewel of the Schönbrunn park: the **Botanischer Garten** (Botanical Garden) with its **Palmenhaus** (palm greenhouse), the largest of its kind in Europe, built of wood and metal by the architect F. von Segenschmid in 1880. In the midst of flower-beds, statues of Franz I and Joseph II and a sundial adorn a delightful corner of the garden which is generally the milieu of children but also of elderly ladies in search of sun and repose.

The Imperial Pavillon and a koala in the Schönbrunn zoo.

Emperor Franz Joseph I and Empress Elisabeth in two paintings by Franz Winterhalter, 1865.

The departure of the royal couple, Franz Joseph and Elisabeth, in a painting in the Wagenburg (ca. 1855).
Below, a view of the Schönbrunn park with the Gloriette.

Wagenburg - In the right wing of the Schönbrunn castle, with its entrance on the Ehrenhof, is the museum exhibiting Imperial coaches and carriages in what was once the castle coach-house. This is the largest collection of vehicles used on State occasions and for pleasure by the Viennese Court between 1690 and 1918. There are coronation coaches, hearses, and hunting and travelling carriages as well as precious trappings and harnesses. Of

The Imperial coronation coach.

special note: the 18th-century **Imperial coronation coach**, **Empress Elisabeth's funeral coach,** and the gig built to order for Napoleon's son.

A few hundred meters from the Schönbrunn castle, at No. 212 at the top of Mariahilfer-Strasse, stands the **Technisches Museum** (Technical Museum): in a three-story building, this museum offers a panorama on the world of technology and industry and on the contribution by Austrian scientists to their development. Among many other exhibits, the first sewing machine (Madersperger, 1830), the oldest typewriter (Mitterhofer, 1860), Cugnot's steam-driven vehicle (1770), and one of the Wright brothers' first airplanes (1903).

Coaches and drays in the Imperial Coach Museum.

Postsparkasse • p. 98

Museum of Applied Arts (MAK) • p. 97

Stadtpark: the Johann Strauss monument • p. 96

Prater • p. 98

Wienflussportal Pavilion • p. 97

The Great Marble Hall • p. 94

The main staircase • p. 95

One of the sphinxes in the Belvedere Park • p. 93

Unteres Belvedere (Lower Belvedere) -
Österreichische Barockmuseum (Museum of Austrian Baroque
Art) - **Belvedere Park** - **Oberes Belvedere** (Upper Belvedere)
- Österreichische Galerie des 19. und 20. Jahrhunderts
(Museum of 19th- and 20th-Century Art) -
Stadtpark - Kursalon - Wienflussportal
(Portal of the River Wien) - **Museum für Angewandte Kunst**
(Austrian Museum of Applied Arts) - Postsparkasse
(Austrian Post Office Savings Bank) - Urania - **Prater**

Museum of 19th- and 20th-Century Art
• p. 95

Museum of
Austrian
Baroque Art
• p. 92

Statue
of Prince Eugene
• p. 92

BELVEDERE CASTLE

HISTORICAL OVERVIEW

In 1683, the Turks laid siege to Vienna for the second time and, as in 1529, the defence of the city became the symbol of Christian resistance against Ottoman expansionism. Even Prince Eugene of Savoy rushed to the aid of the besieged city, offering his services to Emperor Leopold. There thus began a long and magnificent series of battles and victories that made the Prince a well-loved figure throughout the Empire—and one feared by the enemy. He was even supported by the Viennese population when the Emperor attempted to remove him from his position as commander-in-chief of the Imperial armed forces. In that era of glorious wars, Baroque art reached its climax. Its representative powers made it an ideal medium for personifying power, pomp and splendor, and the dominion of absolutism. Even Prince Eugene decided to build a residence for himself near Vienna, of a splendor by no means inferior to that of the Hapsburg royal palace, as a means of confirming his political position. At the same time, every important Baroque building erected meant an alteration to the medieval image of the city; over the decades, this process accelerated until Vienna, from that sort of medieval fortress it had been, became one great Imperial Residence. And thus, in 1714-1716, there was erected the Lower Belvedere, the castle/residence of Prince Eugene. J. Lukas von Hildebrandt, one of the most important architects of the time and the designer of many of the Baroque buildings in Vienna, made the Belvedere a true masterpiece.

At the turn of the 18th century the layout of the Baroque garden was begun; and at the highest point in this panorama of pools and planted beds, Hildebrandt erected the Upper Belvedere in two short years (1721-1722). Following the death of Prince Eugene, the castle passed to the Hapsburgs and in the early years of the 20th century was the residence of the heir to the throne, Archduke Franz Ferdinand, whose assassination in Sarajevo sparked World War I.

View from the Upper Belvedere (Oberes Belvedere) over the garden and Lower Belvedere.

The Lower Belvedere (Unteres Belvedere): the main façade.

Unteres Belvedere - The Belvedere Complex is made up of two buildings separated by the grandiose, gently-sloping, and elegantly designed park. The Lower Belvedere, at the base of the rise, was terminated in 1716 as the residence of Prince Eugene: two simple, low façades conceal a luxurious interior with a series of halls decorated in accordance with the Baroque taste of the era. The **Marble Hall**, frescoed by Martino Altomonte and Gaetano Fanti with scenes celebrating moments of glory in the life of the Prince, merits special attention. To the right of the entrance to the Lower Belvedere is the museum.

Lower Belvedere: the Goldkabinett (or Hall of Mirrors)
with the statue of Prince Eugene by Balthazar Permoser (1721).

Österreichisches Barockmuseum - The Museum of Austrian Baroque Art has found its ideal setting in these 9 rooms. It contains a complete collection of the most important artists and currents in art in the Austria of the 17th and 18th centuries; among the most renowned are J. M. Rottmayr, M. Altomonte, P. Troger, D. Gran, M. J. Schmidt, G. R. Donner, A. Maulbertsch, and F. X. Messerschmidt. Donner was the author of the sculptures adorning the Marble Hall and the Yellow Hall, while the "Character Heads," like the Coward, the Jester, and the Fool, in the Marble Gallery, are the work of Messerschmidt. The museum also houses the lead originals of the statues decorating the Donnerbrunnen (Providentia Fountain) in the Neuer Markt, which represent *Providence* and the four rivers *Enns*, *March*, *Traun*, and *Ybbs*.

Around to the right of the Lower Belvedere we find the Orangery, where masterpieces of late-Gothic panel painting and sculpture are on display in the **Museum Mittelalterlicher Kunst** (Museum of Austrian Medieval Art). The works by Roland Frueauf the Elder (15th century) and other artists are of great interest.

Garden - No great Baroque castle could be considered complete without its park, with a great number of pools, statues, hedges, and avenues and paths in line with the taste of the period. The architectural geometry of the gardens was subject to strict rules. The garden is the work of Dominique Girard (1717): it includes three broadly terraced lawns with fountains, cascades, flights of steps, and statues of figures from Greek mythology that rise to the façade of the Upper Belvedere. A pleasant walk through this fascinating scenario takes us to the Upper Belvedere, which offers a splendid view of Vienna with the Lower Belvedere in the foreground.

Oberes Belvedere - Prince Eugene's summer residence could not have had a more resplendent setting, and here Hildebrandt's artistic expression of the Baroque reached its apex. The long building, with projections and recesses and three series of large windows, it is a convincing statement of harmony and elegance. The Upper Belvedere was not merely a palace for official use; it was also to host great celebrations and entertainments. The entrance hall is of imposing aspect, with vaults supported by four figures of Atlas which give the impression of holding the weight of the entire building on their shoulders. Off the entrance there open

Above, one of the sphinxes in the garden.
Upper Belvedere: the façade on the garden.

The bedroom of Prince Eugene.

a series of salons and the richly decorated staircase leading to the first floor. Here we find the **Chapel** and the **great Marble Hall**, with frescoes by Carlo Carlone. It was in this hall that on 15 May 1955 the four occupying powers and Austria, which guaranteed its independence and neutrality, signed the Austrian State Treaty. In the hall is a painting immortalizing the historic event, a true miracle of diplomacy of the Cold War: the protagonists of the international political scene of the time are easily recognizable.

Upper Belvedere: the Great Marble Hall.
Above, "Character Heads" by Franz Xavier Messerschmidt in the Lower Belvedere.

Upper Belvedere: the main staircase in the entrance hall.

On summer evenings, from May through September, classical "son et lumière" presentations are held, with music, lights, and sound illustrating the fascinating history of the castle and the story of its Prince.

Österreichische Galerie des 19. und 20. Jahrhunderts - The Upper Belvedere today houses an important art gallery containing paintings and sculptures that give us a general idea of the development and flowering of art between the late 19th and early 20th centuries. The artists of the Secession and their art have here been given the prominence they deserve. The Secession artistic movement had begun to develop in open contrast with the official currents in the art of the time. Romako, Makart, and Schindler expressed official artistic leanings; Klimt, Schiele, Kokoschka, Moser, Gerstl, and Hannak are instead only a few of the artists presented in this interesting gallery. On the first floor are

exhibited Secession paintings and sculptures through 1945 (Klimt, Schiele, Kokoschka, Boeckl). On the second floor are portraits and landscapes by painters of the Biedermeier era (F. G. Waldmüller, F. v. Amerling, J. Alt, R. v. Alt, F. Gauermann, and others) besides small paintings by Adalbert Stifter. The works in the Schiele and Klimt collections are quite numerous.

Portrait of Sonia Knips
by Gustav Klimt (1898).

Corpus Christi Morning
by F. G. Waldmüller (1857).

Gustav Klimt

Klimt was born in Vienna in 1862. In 1897 he founded the Viennese Secession, a cultural and artistic movement under the umbrella of European Symbolism. The first phase of Klimt's artistic experience was characterized by two-dimensional style and accentuated linearity; gold is the major color theme in his paintings. Later, the artist abandoned this style of painting, and the gold and elegant lines were replaced by bright, vivacious colors. Klimt died in 1918.

Klimt's first artistic period opened with *Judith I*. The painting is dominated by the figure of the Biblical Judith, represented as a *femme fatale* whose features are probably those of Adele Bloch-Bauer, a matron of Viennese high society. The head of Holofernes is just visible in the lower right corner. *Judith* exasperates that *eros* that leads to blurring the borders between love and death.

STADTPARK

Opened to the public in 1862, this was the first of Vienna's city parks. On its lawns and along the bank of the Wien river are numerous monuments to famous musicians such as *Anton Bruckner* and *Franz Schubert*; the most imposing monument is that dedicated to the *king of waltzes, Johann Strauss*, a work by E. Hellmer. A charming little lake, inhabited by ducks and swans, adorns the center

The Kursalon in the Stadtpark.
Below, the Postsparkasse building.
Facing page, the monument to Johann Strauss and
the Pavilion of the Wienflussportal (Wien River Gate).

of the park. At the westernmost end of the Stadtpark, in the **Kursalon**, an orchestra plays the famous Viennese waltzes every evening from March through October. Strolling along the riverbank, we come to the interesting **Wienflussportal** (Portal of the River Wien), a Jugendstil work by F. Ohmann from 1903-1906.

MUSEUM FÜR ANGEWANDTE KUNST

The Austrian Museum of Applied Arts, built in the years spanning 1868 and 1871, is the oldest of its kind on the European continent. The thousands of pieces of furniture, objects for everyday use, glass, ceramics, rugs, and other items on exhibit in this building on the Stubenring bear mute witness to the high artistic value of handcrafts in different historical periods and in different parts of the globe. Renovation of the MAK exhibits was conducted in collaboration with artists of international fame, who laid out the traditional contents of the collection in a contemporary context.

The exhibits are parcelled out among 10 rooms according to the styles of the different ages: Romanesque, Gothic, Renaissance – Baroque, Rococo – Classicism – Empire, Biedermeier – Historicism, Jugendstil – Oriental Art – Wiener Werkstätte – Jugendstil, Art Déco – Contemporary Art – Eastern Asia. All the sections feature study rooms open to

97

MAK - Austrian Museum of Applied Arts: Biedermeier Imperial Hall.

the public that integrate the exhibit rooms. The valuable MAK collection of glass and porcelain objects, fabrics, and other objects from the Viennese crafts studios is exhibited in an attractive modern setting. From the MAK, past the Stubenring and across to the other bank of the Danube; down Praterstrasse to the Prater. Along the way we find two important Jugendstil buildings. In Georg-Coch-Platz, to the left of the Ring, rises the tall and massive **Postsparkasse** building (Austrian Post Office Savings Bank), a work by the well-known architect Otto Wagner dating from 1904-1905; it was completely renovated in the 1970s and is a typical example of functional architecture: the banking hall is quite interesting. Not far from the Postsparkasse, on the bank of the Donaukanal where the Aspernbrücke unites the first Bezirk (Innere Stadt) with the second Bezirk (Leopoldstadt), is the **Urania** building, built in 1910 by Otto Wagner's protégé Max Fabiani: the Urania is an institute of the Popular University of Vienna with various halls for conferences and movie projection; the tower is home to an astronomical observatory.

PRATER

Not far from the center of the city is the Prater, which can be reached by public transport. In 1560, Emperor Maximilian II transformed this broad stretch of land between the Danube and the Donaukanal into a hunting preserve for exclusive use by the Court and the aristocracy. Two centuries later, in 1766, the illuminated reformer Emperor Joseph II transformed it into an enormous park accessible to the entire population. In just a few years the Prater became the favorite recreation spot for the Viennese. Booths and attractions of all kinds sprang up in ever greater numbers, cafés were opened . . . and the im-

Attractions in the amusement park (Wurstelprater).

The Riesenrad at the Prater

The Ferris Wheel in the Prater park is one of the symbols of Vienna. It was built in 1897 to celebrate the fiftieth year of the reign of the emperor Franz Joseph. In the early 1900's, the Riesenrad was used in several circus spectaculars and in many American film productions. It was destroyed by fire in 1944, and rebuilt at the end of World War II at the same time as the Stephansdom, the Staatsoper, and the Burgtheater. The panoramic ride was reopened to the public in 1947.

Since 2002 the Riesenrad has illuminated the Viennese night, immersed in gold and silver light. Eight of the lost cabins have been found and are now part of a new attraction called "Panorama," which illustrates the history of the wheel and of Vienna.

age of this great extension of woods and meadows was inevitably changed. In the 19th century and until the fall of the monarchy, the Prater was patronized by Viennese of every social extraction. Following its decline during the crisis period spanning the two World Wars and culminating in the destruction wreaked in 1945, the Prater has today regained all its ancient charm. Facilities for a myriad of sports and innumerable attractions stand out in a splendid natural setting.

The **Praterstern**, the vast square at the entrance to the Prater at which the underground stops, is the start of the main boulevard (**Hauptallee**) that divides the Prater in two parts for the five kilometers of its length; at the top of the avenue, on the left, is the **Wurstelprater** (amusement park) with its many cafés and restaurants: a true mecca of rides and booths selling toys and sweets. It is here that one of the symbols of Vienna, the **Riesenrad** (Ferris Wheel), rises to the spectacular height of 64.75 meters. The 15 cars move slowly, at a speed of 75 cm/second, to offer us the opportunity to savor an "aerial" view of the city. The wheel was built in 1897 by the Englishman W. Basset, who had previously designed similar wheels for Chicago, London, Blackpool, and Paris (none of which is still standing). Close by the enormous wheel is the **Pratermuseum**, with its collection of items salvaged from the old amusement park that was razed in 1945.

Not far from the museum are the sports facilities, among which the well-known Vienna Stadium (Ernest-Happel-Stadion).

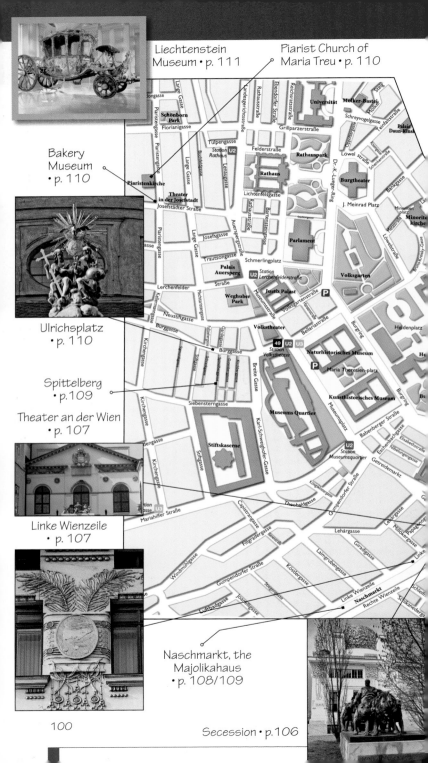

Liechtenstein Museum • p. 111

Piarist Church of Maria Treu • p. 110

Bakery Museum • p. 110

Ulrichsplatz • p. 110

Spittelberg • p.109

Theater an der Wien • p. 107

Linke Wienzeile • p. 107

Naschmarkt, the Majolikahaus • p. 108/109

Secession • p.106

Schönborn Park

Piaristenkirche

Theater in der Josefstadt
Josefstädter Straße

Palais Auersperg

Weghuber Park

Stiftskaserne

Universität

Molker-Bastei

Rathaus

Rathauspark

Burgtheater

J. Meinrad Platz

Minoriten kirche

Parlament

Schmerlingplatz

Justiz Palast

Volksgarten

Volkstheater

Naturhistorisches Museum

Maria Theresien-platz

Kunsthistorisches Museum

Museums Quartier

Heldenplatz

Nelke

Naschmarkt

100

Karlskirche (Church of Saint Charles Borromeo) - Karlsplatz - **Wien Museum Karlsplatz**- Musikvereinsgebäude (Society of the Friends of Music Building) - Künstlerhaus (Artists' House) - Historische Stadtbahnstationen (Historical Underground Pavilions) - *Secession* (Secession Building) - Akademie der Bildenden Künst (Academy of Fine Arts) - **Linke Wienzeile** - Theater an der Wien - Naschmarkt - Flohmarkt (Flea Market) - Majolikahaus - Spittelberg - Barockhaus am Ulrichsplatz - Bäckereimuseum (Bakery Museum) - Piaristenkirche Maria Treu (Piarist Church) - Palais Liechtenstein - Liechtenstein Museum - Josephinum - Sigmund Freud-Haus

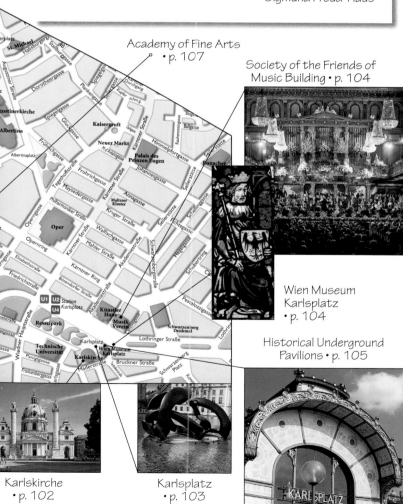

Academy of Fine Arts
• p. 107

Society of the Friends of
Music Building • p. 104

Wien Museum
Karlsplatz
• p. 104

Historical Underground
Pavilions • p. 105

Karlskirche
• p. 102

Karlsplatz
• p. 103

KARLSKIRCHE

In 1713 Vienna was devastated by the plague for the seventh time. Thousands of the city's inhabitants were struck down by the terrible epidemic. Emperor Karl VI, worried over the fate of the city, vowed to raise a church in honor of Saint Charles Borromeo. In 1716, after the plague had been eradicated, the architect J. B. Fischer von Erlach commenced execution of the project, which was completed after his death by his son Joseph Emanuel. The Church of Saint Charles Borromeo is considered a masterpiece of Baroque religious architecture. Seen from the man-made lake where there stands the beautiful but somewhat inadequate sculpture by Henry Moore, *Hill Arches* (1977), the exterior of the church surprises us not only with of its imposing size but also the multiplicity of artistic elements that go to make up the building as a whole.

The Karlskirche.
Details of the dome frescoed by
J. M. Rottmayr and of the interior.

Façade - Two low, heavy towers with large open portals flank the façade. The center staircase, with a statue at each side, leads to the classical six-columned porch behind which the main door opens; on the tympanum, a stucco relief by J. Stanetti shows the *Extinction of the Plague*. The two triumphal columns at the left and the right of the church are the most surprising architectural element in the entire complex: the rich decoration, similar to that of Trajan's Column in Rome, narrates the life of Saint Charles Borromeo, and elegant lanterns crown the summits. The entire construction is dominated by the dome, 72 meters in height.

The **interior** of the church, on an oval plan and in large part realized in marble, is striking thanks to the harmony and the symmetry of the forms and the masterly play of the light created by the large windows of the dome. The *high altar*, built to J. B. Fischer von Erlach's design, with its imposing scenario of gold- and stucco-work, is fascinating. The most capable artists of the time collaborated on the altarpieces: Daniel Gren, Jakob von Schuppen, and Sebastiano Ricci. The fresco in the vault of the towering dome, representing Saint Charles Borromeo supported by the Virgin as he prays for deliverance from the plague, was painted between 1725 and 1730 by J. M. Rottmayr.

KARLSPLATZ

This vast tree-lined square, a short distance from the Ring and linked to the center by Kärntner Strasse, is one of the most significative in Viennese culture, besides being an important city traffic node. Saint Charles' Square is a park with pools and monuments (of note that dedicated to **Johannes Brahms**) and is overlooked by private and institutional buildings that played important roles during the period of Vienna's artistic flowering (19th and 20th centuries). These buildings, together with the Karlskirche, bear witness to the splendor of the former Hapsburg empire. If we stay to the right leaving the church, we come to the Wien Museum Karlsplatz, across from the Künstlerhaus and the Musikverein, as well as to the pavilions of the old underground stations. If we instead turn to the left in the square as we leave the church, toward Wienzeile and the Naschmarkt, we will come to the Secession, stronghold of Viennese Jugendstil.

*The monument to Brahms in the Resselpark.
Above, the sculpture by Henry Moore in Karlsplatz.*

WIEN MUSEUM KARLSPLATZ

The Wien Museum Karlsplatz (until 2003 the City of Vienna Historical Museum), inaugurated in 1959, offers the occasion to make the detailed acquaintance of the history of the city and its development. Subdivided among the three floors of this modern building are exhibits of archaeological finds and objects that narrate over 2000 years of history.

Ground Floor - An overview, from prehistorical times to the 15th century. The section hosts finds and documentary evidence from the Roman garrison of Vindobona, from the Vienna of the Babenbergs, and relating to the building of the great churches (for example, the plans for the Stephansdom and others).

First Floor - Dedicated to the 16th and the 17th centuries. It houses finds and booty from the wars of 1529 and 1683 against the Turks such as suits of armor, weapons, flags, and numerous other objects among which a model of the city when its walls were still standing. There are also paintings and art objects from the 18th century.

Second Floor - Exhibit rooms of the Vienna of the 19th and 20th centuries. A reconstruction of the apartment of F. Grillparzer in the Spiegelgasse, with its original furniture, and paintings and other works by neoclassical artists. Much space is dedicated to the Romanticists and the Jugendstil artists as well as to contemporary painters (Klimt, Kokoschka, Schiele, Hausner, Fuchs, Lehmden, Boeckl). There are also some plastic works by Wotruba and a model of the city in the 19th century after construction of the Ring boulevards.

King Rudolf I. Detail of one of the original stained-glass windows of the Stephansdom (ca. 1390).

MUSIKVEREINSGEBÄUDE

The Society of the Friends of Music building, raised between 1867 and 1869 to plans by Theophil Hansen, has since that time been the center of Viennese musical events. The heart of this large building, which also houses a beautiful collection of musical instruments, is the **Grosse Musikvereinssaal**: 51 meters long by 19 in width, the hall seats 1742 and also provides 300 listening posts. The acoustics of the hall are impeccable and its decoration is magnificent: two rows of gilded caryatids adorn the walls, the ceiling represents Apollo and the nine Muses, and from the great chandeliers sparkle a myriad of

The Grosse Musikvereinssaal.

Johann Strauss

Johann Strauss was born in Vienna in 1825. His father was an acclaimed musician and court orchestra conductor; Johann debuted as orchestra conductor in 1844, to enormous success. He was in competition with his father from the very beginning, and after his father's death he succeeded him as conductor of the music for the court balls.

Johann Strauss is acclaimed as the world's foremost composer of waltzes; he varied the formal structure of the waltz, adding the introduction and the coda. His best-known piece is *An der schönen blauen Donau* ("The Blue Danube"), composed for the Wiener Männersänger-Verein at Carnival 1867. Strauss also wrote many operettas; the best known, still included in many contemporary repertoires, are: *Die Fledermaus, Der Zigeunerbaron, Eine Nacht in Venedig,* and *Wiener Blut.* The composer died in 1899 in Vienna.

points of light; this alone is sufficient to create the resplendent atmosphere of the great events. It is from this hall that the famous New Year's Concert given by the Wiener Philharmoniker is broadcast. The orchestra is one of the world's most celebrated and the Musikverein is its official home. Nearby the Musikvereinsgebäude is the **Künstlerhaus** (Artists' House), completed in 1868; for many years it was the official gallery of the academic artists. In clear-cut contrast with their conservative current there arose the Secession movement, of which Klimt and others were the founders. Today, the Künstlerhaus mainly hosts important temporary exhibitions.

HISTORICAL UNDERGROUND PAVILIONS

On occasion of the building of the new U-bahn during the 1970s, the two pavilions of the Karlsplatz stations of the old underground built by Otto Wagner at the turn of the century were restored. These are two especially suggestive buildings in iron, copper, marble, and gold that reveal a notable eye for detail. One of the two pavilions gives access to the trains of the new underground, while the other hosts a *Kaffeehaus* and a section of the Wien Museum. The two pavilions, together with those of Schönbrunn, Pilgramgasse, Kettenbrückengasse, Stadtpark, and Rossauerlände, are beautiful examples of that Jugendstil architecture of which Otto Wagner was grand master.

The historical underground station by Otto Wagner.

SECESSION

In the year 1897, a group of artists, the most important among whom were Klimt, Moser, Moll, Olbrich, and Hoffmann, formed a new movement in open contrast with the academic artistic currents: it was called Austrian Secession and its aim was to support and promote new directions in art. To this end, a new exhibit building was erected, and the movement elected residence there. The Secession pavilion, built in 1897-1898, was designed by Joseph Olbrich; his is also the **cupola** of gilded iron laurel leaves that surmounts the rigidly geometric structure. The doors were built to designs by Gustav Klimt. On the façade is impressed the motto of the movement: "To Every Age its Art, to Art its Freedom." Alongside the Secession building stands the **Denkmal der Marc-Anton-Gruppe** (Monument to Mark Anthony) by A. Strasser (1899).

Above, the Secession Building and the monument to Mark Anthony.
Detail of the cupola of the Secession buiding.

AKADEMIE DER BILDENDEN KÜNSTE

Right behind Friedrichstrasse, near Karlsplatz, is the beautiful Renaissance Schillerplatz, with at its center the monument to the great poet. On the west side of the square is the Academy of Fine Arts building. The Academy was founded in 1692; since 1876 its headquarters have been in this building by Theophil Hansen. Vienna's is the oldest Academy of Fine Arts in the German-speaking countries and is the only one to possess a **Gemäldegalerie** (picture gallery). Here are found works by the most important artists of the 16th and 17th centuries, including Hieronymus Bosch (*Last Judgment* triptych), Cranach the Elder (*Lucretia*), Rubens (*Circumcision*), Francesco Guardi (*Eight Views of Venice*), Luca Giordano (*The Judgment of Paris*), Memling (*Crucifixion*), Pieter de Hooch (*Dutch Family*), Murillo (*Youths at Dice*), Van Dyck (*Self-Portrait*), and Ruisdael (*Woodland Scene*). The collection also includes works by Tiepolo, Rembrandt, J. Miel, and many other artists mainly of the Flemish and Dutch schools. Modern-day works by Hundertwasser, Boeckl, Weiler, and others are also on exhibit. The Academy boasts an extensive **Drucksammlung** (print collection) of about 100,000 drawings, water-colors, etchings, aquatints, and wood-engravings.

LINKE WIENZEILE

From the Karlsplatz, at the level of the Secession, there begins a long roadway that leads to the Schönbrunn: this is Linke Wienzeile, a popular center of city life, lined with interesting buildings. Just behind the Secession, at No. 6, is the **Theater an der Wien**, inaugurated in 1801, where Beethoven's *Fidelio* was represented for the first time in 1805; numerous other of his works, both serious and comical, were to follow. Today, mainly clas-

Theater an der Wien: the "Papagenotor" (Papageno Portal).

No. 38 Linke Wienzeile, an example of Jugendstil architecture by Otto Wagner. Below, the Naschmarkt.

sical Viennese operettas and operas are staged here. Across from the theater, on the long square that separates the left Wienzeile from the right Wienzeile, the **Naschmarkt** begins: it is a lively, colorful market where groceries, spices, exotic fruits, and macrobiotic foods—in short, something for everyone—are sold. Among the shops and stalls you will also find bars and eating-places. The **Flohmarkt** (Flea Market) is held every Saturday at the end of the Naschmarkt, near the Kettenbrückengasse underground station. It is a typical bazaar of second-hand items, where among the strangest arrays of junk you can sometimes find something very interesting. But attention! If you want to dedicate some of your time to this small but very crowded market, go early: the best pieces are the first to go and latecomers are left with only useless odds and ends.

The ideal spot for a pause after

your visit to the Flohmarkt is the Wienzeile Café, a typical Viennese coffee house that is always very crowded on Saturdays.

Facing the market are two splendid examples of Jugendstil architecture, both designed by the architect Otto Wagner and dating from 1898-1899. At No. 40, the **Majolikahaus**, with its majolica-tile façade in multicolor floral motifs; at No. 38, another private house decorated with gilded medallions after a design by Koloman Moser. The balconies, the wrought-iron doors, and the small columns on the façades of both buildings create an extremely ornamental effect. It is impossible to not feel the lure of such wealth and elegance, in clear contrast with the pompous style of many buildings from the same era.

Detail of the Majolikahaus.

SPITTELBERG

A pleasant stroll through the streets of the 6th and 7th Bezirke (Mariahilf and Neubau) leads us to Spittelberg, an old neighborhood spreading out immediately behind the MuseumsQuartier (Maria-Theresien-Platz). The Spittelberg is a low rise, in front of the ancient fortifications, that was more than once occupied by enemy armies training their artillery on Vienna, like the Turks in 1683 and the French in 1809. The 19th-century expansion of the city embraced the area, which became one of the most ill-famed, with many taverns in which dubious business was conducted. With time, the degradation reached an intolerable level: the authorities were faced with a choice–raze the entire neighborhood or re-vitalize it. Luckily, at the beginning of the 1970s it was decided to take the second line of action, implementation of which produced the results we see today: narrow alleyways with lovely, renovated houses, well-tended courtyards on which well-patronized establishments look out, excellent restaurants, and crafts shops. Certain of the streets in this pedestrian area offer inviting shopping opportunities. The beautiful **Spittelberggasse**, with its various galleries, restaurants, and cafés, is the heart of this neighborhood, which conceals many of its most characteristic sights in charming inner courtyards. One

example is the **Amerlinghaus** at No. 8 Stiftgasse, which hosts an alternative cultural center linked to an inn. In the Burggasse, which delimits the Spittelberg area, we see the rear of the **Ulrichskirche** (Church of Saint Ulrich), built in the years 1721-1724 on the site of an oft-destroyed 13th-century chapel. At No. 2 in the church square stands the noteworthy **Barockhaus** (Baroque House) from the mid-18th century: the richly ornate façade, the splendid courtyard, the balconies, and a small pavilion in the interior lend to the whole a beauty that is rare even in a city like Vienna where Baroque homes are certainly not lacking.

Crossing Lerchenfelderstrasse and proceeding up Lange Gasse leads us to the center of the 8th Bezirk (Josefstadt). A beautiful Baroque house at No. 34 Lange Gasse is home to the Alte Backstube café where the usual connoisseurs meet, but also to the **Bäckereimuseum** (Bakery Museum). Turning down Maria-Treugasse takes us to Jodok-Fink-Platz, the beautiful setting for the Piaristenkirche Maria Treu.

The Plague Column near the Ulrichskirche. Courtyard of a Baroque house on Ulrichsplatz.

PIARISTENKIRCHE MARIA TREU

Built in 1716 to plans by J. Lukas von Hildebrandt, the ochre façade of the beautiful Piarist Church of Maria Treu, set off by two belltowers 76 meters in height, dominates the square. In the interior, the noteworthy *frescoes* of the dome and the ceiling, by Franz Anton Maulbertsch, represent the *Coronation* and the *Assumption of Maria* and some scenes from the Bible. The painting over the tabernacle is a work by J. Herz entitled *Maria Treu*: it was a votive offering in thanks for a miraculous recovery from the plague of 1713 and gives the church its name.

At the center of the square rises a *Mariensäule*, a work by J. Prokop commissioned by a noble in thanks to the Madonna for deliverance from the plague.

PALAIS LIECHTENSTEIN

If we go to the 9th Bezirk (Alsergrund) by car or by trolley (Strassenbahn), we will come to the Liechtenstein Garden Palace, situated between Liechtenstein-strasse and Porzellangasse. Built in 1698-1711 to plans by Domenico Martinelli, it is one of the most beautiful buildings in the city. The simple façade conceals a richly frescoed interior; the frescoes of the medallions in the entrance hall, in the library, in the archives, and on the staircase are by J. M. Rottmayr; the stucco decoration is by S. Bussi and the ceiling frescoes in the Herkulessaal are by A. Pozzo. Since 2004, this building has been home to the LIECHTENSTEIN MUSEUM.

LIECHTENSTEIN MUSEUM – This museum exhibits to the public the private collection of the princes of Liechtenstein, one of the world's most prestigious. The fulcrum of the museum is the picture gallery, with one of the largest collection of Rubens' in the world, and significant works by Lucas Cranach, van Dyck, Rembrandt, and Italian and French artists. There is also a notable sculpture collection, with masterpieces by Sansovino, Susini, and Giuliani.

In addition there are fine porcelains, hunting weapons, and finely-crafted furniture from the castles and palaces of the Liechtenstein princes.

A unique attraction at the museum is the Golden Coach: made for the emperor's ambassador, Prince Joseph Wenzel I of Liechtenstein, it is a French gala coach in Rococo style that survived the French Revolution.

Top, a view of the east staircase of Palais Liechtenstein with frescoes by J. M. Rottmayr (1654-1730).
The south façade of the Liechtenstein Garden Palace.

Prince Joseph Wenzel I of Liechtenstein's golden coach, 1738.
The Death of Decius Mus in Battle *by P. P. Rubens (1616-17).*

JOSEPHINUM

Not far from the Palais Liechtenstein, at No. 25 Wahringer Strasse, we find the 18th-century **Chirurgisch-medizinische Akademie** in the Josephi-num, built by I. Canevale in 1783-1785. The Academy houses the **Museum des Instituts für Geschichte der Medizin** (Museum of the History of Medicine), which includes a large collection of wax anatomical figures ordered by the Emperor Joseph II in 1775 as a learning aid for the surgeons of the Imperial army, who often were not sufficiently expert in providing care to wounded soldiers. These models of the human body with exposed internal organs, or accurately "skinned" in order to reveal the muscles and the vascular system, are the work of Florentine craftsmen (and not by chance, a similar collection is found in Florence). The macabre melancholy of these waxen faces is at once magnetic and highly moving.

SIGMUND–FREUD–HAUS

The home of Sigmund Freud, at No. 19 Berggasse, bears witness to the importance of Vienna in the field of the modern human sciences with the **Sigmund Freud-Museum**, which now occupies the house that the father of psychoanalysis lived in for almost half a century. It was here that Freud developed his revolutionary theories on the psyche and human behavior, until in 1938, with the arrival of Hitler, he was forced to flee Vienna.

Museum of Army History
• p. 114

Hundertwasserhaus
• p. 117

Saint Marx Monumental
Cemetery • p. 118

Central Cemetery • p. 118

Kirche am Steinhof
• p.119

Karl Marx-Hof
• p.120

UNO-City
and Donau City • p. 121

Heurigen
• p. 122

The Donauturm
in Donaupark
• p. 121

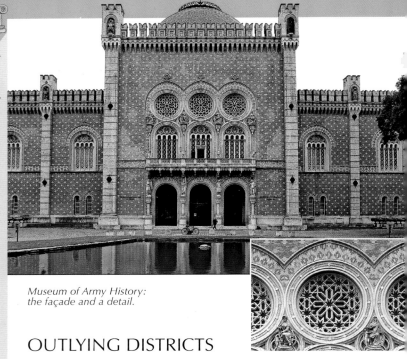

*Museum of Army History:
the façade and a detail.*

OUTLYING DISTRICTS

Heeresgeschichtliches Museum - During the 1848 Revolution, the old arsenal was attacked by the rebels; following this episode, Emperor Franz Joseph decided to build a new fortified arsenal for artillery and a weapons depot outside of the city. The result was a colossal work of military architecture, measuring 688 by 640 meters; the architects were Siccardsburg and Null, the same who designed the Staatsoper.

The cannon aligned in front of the Museum of Army History.

The inner courtyard of the building
housing the Museum of Army History.
Below, the entrance hall.

In the interior of the arsenal was built, to plans by Theophil Hansen, the home of the Museum of Army History. Paintings, weapons, documents, flags, and uniforms breathe life into the history of the Austrian Army from the Thirty Years' War through World War I. Of particular interest, besides the grandiose exhibit of artillery pieces from the 16th through the 18th centuries, is the armor of Prince Eugene, a Turkish tent, a 1796 aerostat, and the automobile in which, on 28 June 1914, Archduke Franz Ferdinand, heir to the Hapsburg throne, fell victim to an assassin in Sarajevo.

Museum of Army History: above, an exhibit of 16th-century armor and 18th century Turkish muskets. On the left, a general's "Hungarian" dress uniform; below, the automobile of the Crown Prince.

Hundertwasserhaus - This original building in the 3rd Bezirk, at the corner of Kegelgasse and Löwengasse, is the work of the internationally famous artist Friedensreich Hundertwasser. Completed in 1985 after two years' work, this fascinating house incorporates many extravagant inventions, including the great variety of colors used and the vivaciously textured external walls with their many different kinds of windows. The multitude of plants on the roofs, the balconies, and the terraces express a close relationship with nature. Not far away, at No. 13 Weissgerberstrasse, is the **Kunsthaus**, a museum dedicated to Hundertwasser and housing many of the master's paintings.

The Hundertwasserhaus.
Design: Univ. Prof. J. Krawina
(TU Berlin), architect; F. Hundertwasser,
painter. Final Project: Arch. Univ. Prof.
J. Krawina, architect; Dl. P. Pelikan.

The memorial to Wolfgang A. Mozart in the St. Marxer Friedhof.

St. Marxer Friedhof - The picturesque Saint Marx cemetery is in Leberstrasse, in the third Bezirk, rather far from the main thoroughfares and almost suffocated by huge viaducts. It was used until the mid-19th century. Today it is more a garden than a cemetery, especially in May when the lilac bushes are in full bloom. It was here that in 1791 Wolfgang Amadeus Mozart was buried in the paupers' grave; his remains were never identified.

Zentralfriedhof - The rapid increase in the population of Vienna during the 19th century made it necessary to build new cemeteries. The Central Cemetery, in the 11th Bezirk (Simmering), was inaugurated in 1874; it soon became one of the most important monumental cemeteries of Europe. From the great Jugendstil gate by Max Hegele (1905), the main boulevard

Church of the Central Cemetery (Zentralfriedhof).

Zentralfriedhof: the monumental tombs of J. Brahms and J. Strauss.

leads us among secular trees to the tombs of major personalities of Austrian culture and politics, among whom Beethoven, Schubert, Brahms, Johann Strauss father and son, Hugo Wolf, Arnold Schönberg, and the Presidents of the Austrian Republic. There is also a monument to Mozart, whose burial place is the nearby cemetery of Saint Marx.

Kirche am Steinhof - This church in the 14th Bezirk, a Jugendstil masterpiece, was erected by Otto Wagner in 1903-1907. Its copper dome strikes us from a distance. In designing this work, Otto Wagner omitted not a single detail: its simple and at the same time elegant lines are set off by geometric white walls while the color gold predominates in the decorative motifs and portraits that embellish its interior. The *stained-glass windows* by Koloman Moser are also exquisitely beautiful.

Kirche am Steinhof: the façade and a view of the interior with the mosaic above the high altar.

Donau City and UNO-City.

Karl Marx-Hof - In the interval between the two World Wars, the socialist municipal government of Vienna instituted a policy of popular residential development in order to resolve the pressing problem represented by the housing shortage. Of the 64,000 apartments built in that period, a predominant part is located in the Karl Marx-Hof residential complex in the 19th Bezirk (Döbling). The more than 1300 apartments are home to over 5000 people. With its long façade (1200 meters) broken by six towers, the Karl Marx-Hof is the symbol of the so-called "Red Vienna" of the Twenties; it is considered a statement of Expressionist architecture influenced by Cubism and Art Déco. The gigantic complex, built between 1927 and 1930, is integrated by wooded areas. It was designed by Karl Ehn, a pupil of Otto Wagner.

The Karl Marx-Hof.

On the right, the Donauturm.

Donau City – Vienna Donau-City, directly on the Danube, is one of the most modern complexes in the city and one of Austria's most brilliant development projects. This project is of particular importance due to its proximity to the Vienna International Center (UNO-City) and the presence of the Austria Center Vienna. Vienna Donau-City is a recreational and cultural center with offices, apartments, and educational and research institutions.

UNO-City - This center is the symbol of Austria's neutrality and her role as mediator between East and West and North and South. The gigantic steel, glass, and cement complex, situated in the 22nd Bezirk, was built in 1973-1979; its countless offices are the headquarters of a myriad of international organizations such as the United Nations Atomic Energy Commission, UNI-DO, and the Center for Social Progress and Human Rights. Situated near the Danube and the extensive park of the same name, UNO City is composed of four buildings, 120, 100, 80, and 60 meters in height, and boasts a total of 24,000 windows.

Donaupark - This territory assigned to the 22nd Bezirk (Donaustadt), lying between the Danube and the "Old Danube," was transformed after 1964 into a beautiful park with man-made lakes, areas featuring children's amusements, skating rinks, and cycle paths, all immersed in a green setting. The park also hosts the **Donauturm**, 252 meters in height, built in 1964 on the model of other television transmission towers on occasion of the Vienna International Garden Show. High-speed elevators take visitors to the revolving café-restaurant, 170 meters above ground level, which offers a marvelous view of Vienna and its surroundings.

HEURIGEN

The word "Heurigen" derives from the expression "Heuriger Wein" (new wine, this year's wine) and denotes the establishments that serve this drink. These are usually found outside of the city, where the vineyards reign unchallenged, and are very often managed by the owners of the wineries themselves. The characteristic sign of the Heurigen is a bough of Scotch pine hanging outside. Here we can eat, drink and listen to music (above all popular music and the Viennese Lieder) in a special atmosphere that is held in high esteem by both Viennese and tourists alike. Heurigen are found in a number of districts within the city limits; some of the best-known are listed below.

Grinzing, in the 19th Bezirk (Döbling), has become famous around the world for its lantern-lit streets, its picturesque corners, its enchanted feeling. More than 30 Heurigen are situated here. Leaving Grinzing, the Cobenzlgasse takes us to the Hohenstrasse, which winds along the slopes of the

Above, the cosy atmosphere of the Heurigen.
A picturesque alley in Grinzing.

The romantic Wienerwald (Vienna Wood).

Wienerwald (Vienna Wood), touches Kahlenberg and runs through Leopoldsberg on to Klosterneuberg. The name **Kahlenberg** is linked to the victory over the Turks by the Imperial troops, allied with the King of Poland Johann III Sobieski, in 1683. A broad panoramic terrace on the roof of a restaurant not far from the 18th century Josephskirche offers a splendid view of Vienna and the Danube valley. Another superb panorama is that from the square of the small church of **Leopoldsberg**, looking out over the Danube. The church was built in 1679 by Leopold I.

The Kahlenberg church.

Beethoven's house in Heiligenstadt.

Heiligenstadt - Nussdorf - These are two more Döbling suburbs in which are situated suggestive Heurigen, favorite destinations for excursions. Ludwig von Beethoven lived in Heiligenstadt off and on between 1802 and 1824; certain of the houses he inhabited are still standing.

Stammersdorf, on the opposite bank of the Danube in the 21st Bezirk (Floridsdorf), arises in the midst of the largest extension of vineyards in the environs of Vienna. Here are located about 100 wineries, many with their own Heurige.
In the Hagenbrunnerstrasse, a true "Kellergasse" (street lined with wine-cellars), we are literally immersed in unique atmosphere of the Heurigen.
Other typical establishments of this type can be found in the outskirts of the city, in Strebersdorf, Sievering, Neusift am Walde, Hernals, Ottakring, Mauer, and Oberlaa (which is also a health center and spa).

The parish church of Heiligenstadt
and the Leopoldskirche of Leopoldsberg.

VIENNESE CUISINE

Viennese gastronomy has been strongly influenced by the cuisines of the various peoples governed by the Austro-Hungarian Empire, and therefore its dishes are not just Austrian but incorporate Italian, Hungarian, and Bohemian elements. Two dishes, in particular, show this amalgam of traditions: Wiener Schnitzel, adopted from Milan, and Viennese goulash, a variant of the typical Hungarian dish. Beef-based dishes, and Wiener Tafelspitz in particular, can be found in any menu. The sweets are unequalled anywhere: Vienna offers a vast assortment of cakes, Strudeln, and other sweets; the Sachertorte is undoubtedly the best known.

Besides high-end restaurants, Vienna abounds in Beisln, typical eating houses with plain decor that offer typical Viennese dishes. In the many coffee houses you can enjoy the exquisite Viennese pastries and cakes with an excellent cup of coffee. In Vienna you'll find this drink served in at least ten different versions: Turkish coffee, Mélange (café au lait with whipped cream), a large or small Brauner (strong coffee with milk), a large or small Schwarzer (without milk), diluted Brauner or Schwarzer (like the above, but with more water), and even a coffee recipe with raw egg yolk and brandy!

WIENER SCHNITZEL

(Viennese Breaded Cutlet)

Veal or pork cutlet (the classical Wienerschnitzel is made with veal), sprinkled with salt, dipped in flour, beaten egg, and finally Brösel (bread crumbs). It is pan-fried in lard until golden. We recommend serving this entrée with lemon wedges and Viennese potato salad.

SACHERTORTE

The "Original Sachertorte" name is a registered trademark of Vienna's Hotel Sacher; the recipe is a well-kept secret. Until 1965 the rights in the name were contested with the Demel pastry-shop, which since it was founded has been producing an "original Viennese Sachertorte." Demel's Sachertorte differs from the "Original Sachertorte" in having its apricot jam filling under the chocolate icing and not between the layers of the cake.

INDEX

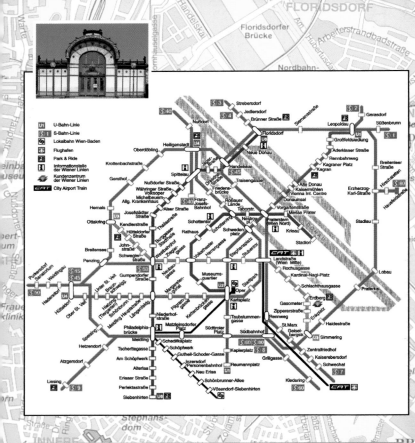

MuseumsQuartier

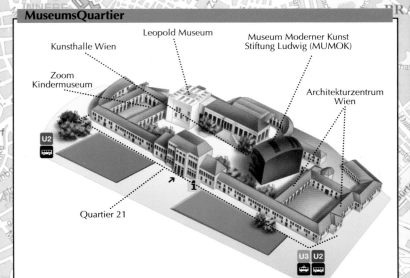

Kunsthalle Wien

Leopold Museum

Museum Moderner Kunst
Stiftung Ludwig (MUMOK)

Zoom
Kindermuseum

Architekturzentrum
Wien

Quartier 21